Soviet Socialist Realism: Origins and Theory

Soviet Socialist Realism

Origins and Theory

C. VAUGHAN JAMES

Senior Fellow in Language Studies in the University of Sussex

St. Martin's Press   New York

AFFILIATED PUBLISHERS: Macmillan Limited, London –
also at Bombay, Calcutta, Madras and Melbourne

Contents

List of Plates

Agitation and propaganda acquire special edge and efficacy when decked in the attractive and powerful forms of art.

Arts Section, Narkompros
& Rabis, 1921

In conformity with the interests of the working people and in order to strengthen the socialist system, the citizens of the USSR are guaranteed by law :

(*a*) freedom of speech;

(*b*) freedom of the press;

(*c*) freedom of assembly, including the holding of mass meetings;

(*d*) freedom of street processions and demonstrations.

These civil rights are ensured by placing at the disposal of the working people and their organisations printing presses, stocks of paper, public buildings, the streets, communications facilities and other material requisites for the exercise of these rights.

Constitution of the USSR 1936
(Article 125)

Agitation and propaganda conducted for the purpose of overthrowing or weakening Soviet authority or for the commission of single especially dangerous state crimes; the distribution for these same purposes of slanderous inventions against the Soviet state and public structure, and also the distribution or preparation of or possession for these same purposes of literature having such a content shall be punished by deprivation of freedom for a term of from 6 months to 7 years or exile for a term of from 2 to 5 years.

Law on Criminal Responsibility for
State Crimes, 25 December 1958

Introduction

THE Western reader of Soviet literature is faced with a number of problems at several levels. Quite apart from the linguistic barrier, the inaccessibility of sources, the lack of documentation and research, and the piecemeal nature of most treatments, with the political attitudes that often invest them, he encounters a whole philosophy that Lénin, its prime architect, described as 'alien and strange to the bourgeoisie and bourgeois democracy'.[1] Brought up in a society that not only does not boast a widely-accepted theory of the socio-political function of art but is, in the main, hostile to the very idea of the elaboration of such a theory, he is thrown into dramatic confrontation with the 'artistic method' of Socialist Realism. This, he learns, 'demands from the artist a true and historically concrete depiction of reality in its revolutionary development. Moreover, this true and historically concrete depiction of reality must be combined with the task of educating the workers in the spirit of Communism.'[2] His bewilderment as to what this formula might mean will be rendered even greater by being informed (as the reader of almost any Western history of Soviet literature will be) that no less a personage than Mikhaíl Shólokhov, winner of the Nobel Prize for literature and author of the universally admired novels *The Quiet Don* (*Tíkhy Don*) and *Virgin Soil Upturned* (*Pódnyataya tseliná*), himself once proclaimed himself unable to say what Socialist Realism was.[3] Yet without some unravelling of this mystery the student will at best not completely understand, and at worst positively misunderstand, a great deal of what he reads, hears or views.

Of course, the Western reader may prefer to judge Soviet writing only by the 'universal' criteria by which he judges other literature; but an important critical dimension may well be thought lacking if such writing is not also regarded from the point of view of the explicit aesthetic criteria of the society in which the author lives and writes. Certainly, any understanding of the *scandales* concerning such authors as Pasternák, Sinyávsky, Daniél or Solzhenítsyn in anything but the crudest political terms is rendered doubly difficult in the absence of detailed points of reference in the sense of a grasp not only of the 'formula' of Socialist Realism but of the principles that underlie it and, at least to some extent, of the history of their evolution. The object of this present study is to contribute – however modestly – to providing a basis for such understanding and hence for independent judgement.

Such an aim has naturally dictated much of the content of this book, in which I have set out to present, in Chapters 1 (Art and the People) and 4 (Socialist Realism), a brief but fairly comprehensive survey of the Soviet point of view. For this purpose I have made extensive use of Soviet sources, in Russian, so that the arguments presented are those with which the Soviet student is himself confronted. In these chapters I have restricted my own comments to a minimum, and though my own convictions must inevitably have influenced both my selection of material and its presentation, I am confident that the reader will have little difficulty in applying any necessary corrective interpretation.

Chapter 1 is a discussion of certain basic principles of Soviet aesthetics, and Chapter 4 is a description of Socialist Realism which relies for its clarity on a knowledge of those principles. Together they make up a coherent whole, representing a summary of official Soviet attitudes since the death of Stálin in 1953. But whereas Chapters 1 and 4 are largely descriptive, Chapters 2 and 3 are analytical and historical. A quite vital element in the aesthetic system on which the method of Socialist Realism is based is the principle of the writer's allegiance to the Communist Party (*partiinost'*), which is extrapolated from Lénin's 1905 article, 'Party Organisation and Party Literature', and vigorous arguments rage as to whether or not such extrapolation is justified. In Chapter 2, therefore, I have tried to follow through the Soviet line of reasoning, though not here refraining from making my own comments or drawing my own conclusions, and the theme is taken up again in Chapter 3.

Two quite distinct theories of the origin of Socialist Realism are widespread. To its opponents, it is the extension into the cultural field of Stalinist policies as they may be observed in other branches of social life. This means that Socialist Realism was invented by Stálin, Zhdánov and Górky and forced on the unwilling artists in the early thirties by the formation of the artistic unions, beginning with the Union of Soviet Writers in 1934. From such a point of view, Socialist Realism derives from the 1930s and is in origin Russian and Stalinist.

To the proponents of Socialist Realism, however, it is a world-wide development, though with local peculiarities, associated with the rise of a politically conscious, i.e. Marxist, industrial proletariat. It is therefore the reflection in the arts of the battle for the creation of a socialist society. It obviously dates in each country from the emergence of a Marxist proletarian movement; in Russia the crucial date was 1895. The theory – as opposed to the tendency in art – was not elaborated or given a name until 1932–4, but it was then simply a summary and codification of what had already been evolving for several decades, strengthened by the Marxist-Leninist understanding of social developments and consequent ability to shape and foretell the future. From such a viewpoint it is in origin Leninist, and what happened in the thirties in the USSR was not a logical stage but a temporary aberration.

This is not a mere quibble, since its implications for the whole history of the arts in the USSR are clearly very grave; Socialist Realism is either a thing of the past or of the present and future. I have therefore examined some of the evidence for the period between the 1917 October Revolution and the announcement of the formation of the artists' unions in 1932 and have drawn what seems to me the inescapable conclusion. Chapter 2, which deals with Lénin's analysis of the three periods of the Russian revolutionary movement as applied to the arts, aims to throw some light on the subject but is, of necessity, inconclusive. Chapter 3 is a quite detailed analysis of party statements on the arts and related topics throughout the twenties: if the theory of Socialist Realism as proclaimed in 1934 contradicted previous attitudes, then there was a case for the 'Stalinist' argument; if not, and a direct line could be traced back to Lénin's own pronouncements, then the contrary argument would seem the more convincing.

The case for the 'official' Soviet version of the origin of Socialist Realism rests on three major arguments: that Socialist Realism in art is a logical development of nineteenth-century realism; that the principle of allegiance to the Party is properly attributable to Lénin; and that the theory as formulated in the thirties was firmly rooted in the practice of the twenties. These arguments, in turn, rest upon certain documentary evidence: for the relationship with previous epochs – Lénin's 1912 speech 'In Memory of Hérzen'; for the principle of allegiance to the Party – Lénin's 1905 article 'Party Organisation and Party Literature'; and for policy and attitudes in the twenties – the Central Committee's resolutions and decisions throughout that period. Space for all these documents was obviously not available to us in this volume, but as Appendices we have included translations of Lénin's 1912 speech and 1905 article, and of documents on the Proletkults (1920), the Central Committee's resolution 'On the Party's Policy in the Field of Literature' (1925), and its decision 'On the Reformation of Literary-Artistic Organisations' (1932). It is hoped that within the context of the arguments put forward in Chapters 2 (Art and the Party) and 3 (A Few Decrees . . .) these will assist the reader to draw his own conclusions. Other party statements from the 1920s are discussed in Chapter 3 at some length since they are not, as far as I know, available in English nor – indeed – are they easily obtained in Russian. Unless otherwise stated, the translation of all documents and extracts is my own, as are italics marked with an asterisk.

The reader who follows Soviet literary affairs as reflected in the Western press may well feel inclined to comment that in this book I have spent very little time discussing such well-known names as those of Pasternák, Sinyávsky, Daniél and Solzhenítsyn. It is quite true that they figure very little in the text; yet in a sense the entire book is about them. For each of them in some way and to some degree either failed to observe or chose to disregard one or several of the canons of Socialist Realism and in so doing incurred the displeasure of the Union of Writers and the Communist Party. Each of them questioned or rejected some element in the theory of the role of the artist in society, the individual in the collective, the intellectual in the mass. It is my belief that although the study of exceptions may tell us a great deal about the norm, the reverse is also true. A study of the 'dissidents' is clearly illuminating; but our understanding of them can only be deepened by a study of the philosophy from which they dissent. My aim has not been to discount the celebrated names which have become so familiar; rather has it been to embrace the countless others of whom the average reader never hears.

There are many ironies in the Soviet situation. Thus a sad legacy of Stalinist days is that the very appellation 'socialist realism' tends to be taken almost automatically as referring to something wholly negative, though the socialist dream of a better reality continues to inspire millions. And 'socialist realism' is similarly taken to mean the total negation of artistic experimentation, though it is itself an artistic experiment on an unprecedented scale. For not only is it an attempt to enlist the poet as philosopher, the writer as tribune and the artist as teacher in the translation of the socialist dream into reality, but it explores the almost unknown interstices between artistic genres by uniting poet, painter, sculptor, singer, actor, dancer and director in one common socio-aesthetic system. And as the fearful problems of the 1920s that faced an isolated revolutionary regime clinging grimly to power over a largely illiterate populace, hungry for bread as well as circuses, become with the passage of time less awesome, there are signs that the purely restrictive aspects of Socialist Realism may be giving way at last to the more creative elements. But its history has been a chequered one: whenever a theory is elaborated to regulate an evolving situation, then one of two things must surely happen; either the theory must itself evolve – in which case it may come near to contradicting itself, or, if it remains rigid, it will become a bar to progress and a force for conservatism. It is arguable that the 'method' of Socialist Realism has exhibited both these characteristics even, on occasion, at one and the same time.

* * *

For readers who are unfamiliar with the Russian language, the pronunciation of names is frequently something of a problem. I have attempted to lessen this by using a form of transliteration in the body of the text which, while not entirely consistent, is scientific without being pedantic. And on commonly-used names, etc. I have marked the stressed syllables with an acute accent (e.g. Mayakóvsky) and the letter ё, pronounced [o] or [yo] (e.g. Khrushchëv).

I should like to thank my Sussex colleagues Beryl Williams, Robin Milner-Gulland and Christopher Thorne for their interest and advice, Hazel Ireson for deciphering my script, and my publishers for their tolerance and support.

Ditchling, Sussex   C.V.J.

1 Art and the People

SOCIALIST REALISM, described by Soviet critics as an 'artistic method', is supported by a corpus of highly complicated theory which, though it receives little attention in Western commentaries, is the subject of voluminous writing inside the USSR. It embraces a number of important questions: the evolution of art – the organic relationship between the art of the past and the art of the present and future; the class nature of art – its objective reflection of social relations; and the function of art in society – the obligations of the artist to the society in which he works, and hence the relationship between the artist and the politician. Moreover it considers the didactic potential of art and its relationship in this sense with the mass communication media in a modern, industrialised society. It therefore concerns every aspect of intellectual life, and it seems not unreasonable to suggest that it is the essential key to an understanding of the artistic life of the Soviet Union today. In particular it is the natural basis for a discussion of literature and politics.

But a necessary preliminary to such a discussion is a clarification of terms, especially since many of them will be new to the Western reader. We shall consequently begin our discussion of Socialist Realism by examining three basic principles of Soviet aesthetics – naródnost' (literally people-ness) – the relationship between art and the masses, klássovost' (class-ness) – the class characteristics of art, and partíinost' (party-ness) – the identification of the artist with the Communist Party of the Soviet Union (CPSU). These are awkward terms to translate, and we have not thought it necessary to do so, especially as two of them are based on familiar borrowings.

The three principles, though stemming ultimately from Marxist theory, are essentially Leninist, and it is important to stress at the very outset of our discussion that here, as perhaps in Marxism-Leninism in general, it is the latter element that is dominant. It was in the glosses that he insisted on putting on the words of Marx and Engels that Lénin differed from his Marxist contemporaries who, especially Plekhánov, were certainly of no lesser stature as political philosophers than he was.

This need not necessarily lead us to conclude that it was Lénin's personal and somewhat conservative tastes that determined the course of development of Soviet arts. It seems unlikely that even Lénin (who in his day was hardly less powerful than Stálin was later to become) could have inflicted his own views on so many of the party intellectuals if they had not in fact been already quite closely in tune. Certainly such cultured and influential figures as Lunachársky had strong and sophisticated attitudes which, though they might occasionally have been upset by some modish fancy or have differed from Lénin's on matters of detail (and we shall mention more than one such occasion in the course of our investigation), coincided nevertheless with his on the one important point – their evaluation of the cultural heritage of the pre-revolutionary era.

This was the crucial point. It may seem paradoxical that the revolutionary leaders who seemed intent on sweeping the old order off the face of the globe and transforming 'reality' in its entirety should have been so adamant in protecting the cultural heritage from their own followers, inisisting (as indeed they may ultimately be seen to have done in many other spheres) on the essential continuity of artistic traditions. Yet this was the keystone of the policy that emerged in the 1920s, and this is what gives Socialist Realism its paradoxical but inescapable air of *déjà vu*.

The policy rests, in the first instance, on the principles of *naródnost'* and *klássovost'*, and in the following paragraphs we have attempted to present the sort of explanation of them that a Soviet critic himself makes. It is perhaps not surprising that except for certain points of detailed interpretation, there is little disagreement amongst orthodox Soviet theoreticians.[1] Nevertheless it seemed wise to select one authority for the exposition of the Soviet view, remembering that since our object is to examine that view, such an authority becomes in fact a primary source. Readers familiar with Soviet criticism will appreciate the problem involved in reducing lengthy and often convoluted arguments into brief and clear statements; such, however, is the object of this chapter.

The authority selected is *Bases of Marxist-Leninist Aesthetics* (*Osnóvy marksístsko-léninskoi estétiki*), 1960 edition, published by the State Publishers of Political Literature, Moscow, Institutes of Philosophy and History of Art of the Academy of Sciences of the USSR and edited by A. Sutyágin. This publication is intended for home consumption, and an important part of the argument is the evidence adduced from the Marxist classics. Such references are therefore reproduced here, though much abbreviated. The date of the edition is significant, since it marked a high point of the Khrushchëv era, when the process of de-Stalinisation was leading to a re-examination and restatement of attitudes. Other useful sources are the series of textbooks published by various Soviet universities, both for their own students and for foreigners, especially from the 'third world'. Unfortunately there are no such publications in English, since the language of instruction is Russian. It is therefore hoped that the following pages will represent a faithful summary of the argument and will go some way to make up for the lack. To distinguish the summary from the rest of my text, the relevant paragraphs are set in smaller print and preceded by an asterisk.

I

* A central position in Marxist-Leninist aesthetics is occupied by the problem of *naródnost'*, which is described as the meeting point of artistic quality, ideological content and social function. It is the point of intersection of a number of forces which characterise the position of art in pre-class, class and classless society. 'It is through *naródnost'* that the significance of art for the whole of mankind becomes especially apparent.' [2]

* Works of art which may be categorised as 'popular' (*naródny*) [3] are those which give strong expression to the highest level of social awareness attained in a given epoch, that is, works which are a compound of the thought, feelings and social moods of the epoch, a reflection of true social conditions and of man's most humane aspirations in his struggle for a more dignified mode of existence. Thus *naródnost'* is the quality that determines the relationship between art and the epoch.

* However, not all the features that relate art to a given epoch are genuinely 'popular'. Thus quantitative features, such as the degree to which certain artistic phenomena are widespread at a given moment do not guarantee a genuinely 'popular' nature. [4] In both social content and artistic form, works become 'popular' only when the social and aesthetic ideals upon which they rest are expressions of the most progressive tendencies of the times. Truly 'popular' works may even appear ahead of their time, for they include elements which, though born of a given epoch, contain the essence of what must develop in the future.

* Thus works that embody the highest degree of *naródnost'* for their times acquire an aspect of transferability and preserve their worth for subsequent epochs. In this sense, art constitutes a material monument to man's persistent aspiration toward a higher stage of development for both himself and society. The great art of past times enriches all men, losing its parochial nature and becoming universal. By virtue of its 'popular' aspect, the art of one people may become part of the heritage of others, who therefore become aware of the universal significance of the most advanced ideals for the whole of mankind.

* All great art is handed down from one generation to another as part of the cultural heritage. Architectural monuments become part of the life of later epochs and exert a formative influence on artistic taste; [5] folk music

retains a peculiar emotional impact throughout the history of a people; myths and legends become part of the popular consciousness. All these contribute to a people's cultural development and are a constant source of aesthetic pleasure. But it is not only collective culture that may become universal; the works of individual artists may also acquire universality by virtue of their *naródnost'*. However, no degree of talent will produce a genuine work of art unless the artist is guided by what is vital to society, that is, unless his work is rooted in the life of the people.

* *Naródnost'* may manifest itself in different ways and in different forms, depending on conditions in the development of the culture of the times. The plays of Aeschylus, Gothic architecture, the works of Goethe and Púshkin, Daumier and Répin, Mayakóvsky and Shólokhov all share the quality of *naródnost'*, though in different ways. To clarify these differences, we must refine the concept of *naródnost'* in the context of class society.

* The most important factor is the relationship between a work of art and the society in which it is produced. The complex and contradictory ways in which *naródnost'* appears result from the contradictions inherent in society, for no society is homogeneous; all societies are composed of classes.

* In very primitive societies this was not so, and in such societies art had a genuinely 'popular' character. But the rise of capitalism and consequent development of classes led to a rift between spiritual and physical activities and hence between the masses and art. Whereas in feudal society 'medieval craftsmen still had a certain interest in their work and in skill in performing it, and this interest could rise to the level of primitive artistic taste',[6] men working under duress in a capitalist system find their work a sheer burden, and hence lose any interest in art. 'Deprived of the possibility of doing anything independently or appropriate to his natural gifts, the labourer in a manufacturing job develops his productive activity merely as an appendage of the capitalist's workshop.'[7] The division of labour destroys the organic unity of spiritual and material activities of primitive society, resulting in a divorce of art from the masses and of the masses from art.

* In such circumstances art develops along two distinct lines. On the one hand folk art lives on in songs, dances and decorative skills. On the other hand there is a development of professional, individual art in all its riches, but this is accessible to only a limited section of society, in general to the ruling classes. However, this does not mean that professional art is devoid of *naródnost'*. It is even possible that it is the most progressive representatives of such art that convey the fullest reflection of the life and fundamental interests of the people. This was true of Russian democratic culture in the nineteenth century, as witnessed in the works of Chernyshévsky and Nekrásov in literature and Répin and Súrikov in painting. Therefore the *naródnost'* of individual art, though it develops in a context of the contradictions engendered by class society, may nevertheless be the most important artistic vehicle by which the ideals of the people are expressed.

* Bourgeois society engenders 'art for art's sake', that is, art for artists. Bourgeois ideologists consider this to be inevitable and proper; for them, good art is always intelligible only to an elite. But progressive ideologists have always held that art has point only when it is accessible to the people,

both by its content and in its aesthetic value. Art that is not accessible to the masses is bad art.

* This problem was correctly defined in the eighteenth century by Jean-Jacques Rousseau, but he, like Tolstóy in the nineteenth century, was unable to postulate the correct solution. By denying the aesthetic worth of elitist art he displayed his inability to see that in a society riven with class antagonisms progressive art is nevertheless 'popular', since it ultimately represents the interests of the working masses. Rousseau's influence is clearly visible in German idealist aesthetics, especially of Schiller and Hegel; but whereas Rousseau, in the interests of equality, wished to sacrifice the benefits of elitist art, Schiller's aim was to elevate mankind as a whole to a level at which they could be appreciated, though his approach was too idealistic and far removed from reality. Hegel, in his 'Aesthetics', raised a whole series of problems related to *naródnost'* and stated quite categorically that 'art does not exist for a small, exclusive circle, a restricted group of highly educated men; it exists entirely for the whole people.'[8] But he, too, was unable to see the development of universal art in correct perspective.

* To a certain extent Rousseau's ideas were adopted by the romantic movement, but the more reactionary romantics developed them in quite a different way. In the early stages of the movement the ideology of the romantics was a reaction against the French revolution and the Enlightenment. But whereas for the latter the principle of *naródnost'* was related to the general aims of the bourgeois democratic movement of the epoch, the romantics looked for their ideal toward the feudal society of the Middle Ages. Realising the incompatibility of capitalism with beauty, they turned to the religion of the Catholic Church (Chateaubriand) or idealised the Age of Chivalry (Schlegel). Their concept of *naródnost'* was therefore reactionary, and this is reflected also in their aesthetic ideals. The revolutionary romantics, on the other hand, looked toward the republicanism of antiquity for their ideal, so for them *naródnost'* demanded civic equality and social liberty. The revolutionary *naródnost'* of their utopian socialism found its most vivid expression in Shelley's 'The Defence of Poetry'.

* Thus in eighteenth and nineteenth century thought great progress was made towards revealing the contradictions in the development of art in a class society and the central problem was that of the accessibility of art to the masses. Even so there was a failure to penetrate to the essence of the contradictions and to comprehend the way in which progressive art in a capitalist society may nevertheless be 'popular'. The Russian revolutionary democrats moved a long way along this path, but only Marxism could provide the explanation of the *naródnost'* of progressive art by linking it with the theory of socialist revolution, which resolves, in particular, the problem of the rift between the masses and art.

* Marx and Engels showed that the creation of a social system in which the masses would be able to develop their spiritual and artistic faculties to the full necessitated the complete transformation of society through socialism. Only a socialist system could provide the conditions in which 'everyone in whom a Raphael lies hidden must have the opportunity of untrammelled development'.[9] In such a society the development of advanced industrial

techniques would not operate, as the romantics had suggested, against the interests of art; on the contrary, it would afford every member of society ample leisure and facilities for the development and enjoyment of the arts.[10]

In nineteenth century Russia, the critic Dobrolyúbov demonstrated that the precious 'popular' elements in the works of the great prose writers of the times were essentially inaccessible to the masses,[11] and the poet Nekrásov dreamed of the time when the peasant would return from the market with the works of Belínsky and Gógol in his bag.[12] In the twentieth century Lénin took up the theme, laying the foundations of subsequent Soviet policy: '... Art must have its deepest roots in the very depths of the broad masses of the workers. It must be understood by those masses and loved by them. It must unite the feelings, thoughts and will of the masses and raise them up. It must arouse the artists among them and develop them.[13]

2

We have seen that in a class society art develops along two distinct lines, reflecting the dichotomy in the society itself. Folk art continues to develop amongst the masses, but the ruling classes develop professional, individual or academic art which is to varying degrees inaccessible to those masses. We must now define what role is played by *naródnost'* in each of these two kinds of art and the relationship between them.

* This question was much discussed amongst the ideologists of the Enlightenment, who represented two rather conflicting points of view. Proceeding from the general proposition that art should develop on the basis of the ideas and forms worked out in the popular consciousness, Lessing nevertheless did not consider that this meant a return to primitive forms. For him, the artist should combine elements of folk art with the most progressive ideas and in his working out of popular subjects and themes he should make use of the entire battery of artistic techniques evolved throughout the ages. By so doing he carries *naródnost'* on to a higher plane. Rousseau, on the other hand, thought it necessary to return to the primitive art forms preserved in the masses. Thus folk poetry was superior to the work of individual poets, who should therefore adopt the folk forms. This belief did in fact exert a partly beneficial influence in the late eighteenth and early nineteenth centuries, but it remains untrue that only the traditional folk arts may be termed 'popular'.

* The nineteenth century Russian revolutionary democrats analysed the problem of *naródnost'* in great detail, demonstrating, in particular, the role it plays in art that does not proceed directly from the masses. Of especial importance in this context is the work of V. G. Belínsky (1811–48), the first great theorist of Russian realism.

* Belínsky defined two distinct periods in the history of every people – an early, instinctive period and a later, conscious period. In the first the national peculiarities of the people are more sharply expressed and its poetry is therefore highly individual to it and consequently inaccessible to other peoples.

Hence, for example, the sharp emotional impact of Russian folk songs on Russians and the difficulty of conveying this impact to non-Russians. But in the second period poetry attains a higher level of sophistication, becomes less accessible to the masses, but is proportionately more accessible to other peoples.[14] This second kind of poetry is always superior to the first, which is the 'childish prattle' of an as yet inarticulate people. The poetry of the second period is articulate and refined and achieves a balance between form and content by evolving forms appropriate to the ideas embodied in them. The highest degree of *naródnost'* is found in art that reflects the basic interests of the masses and develops the most progressive ideas of the epoch. 'Popular' art is art which facilitates the progress of society along the path to freedom.

* Belínsky's assessment of Púshkin is a good example of his approach; Púshkin understood the impossibility of resorting to slavish imitation of folk poetry in academic art, but he nevertheless enriched his own poetry from that source, and by his link with the revolutionary movement of the epoch he exerted a great influence on progressive thought. Such an appraisal does not in any way imply denigration of folk poetry, which possesses a quality 'that cannot be replaced by academic poetry'.[15]

* An essential aspect of Belínsky's two periods is that the second is an organic development of the first. Thus academic poetry embodies elements of folk poetry, with its own overlay. It is a conscious development of earlier forms which, though the period in which they arose may be long since past, still continue to provide aesthetic pleasure.

* While largely sharing Belínsky's attitude to folk art, Marx offered a different solution of the problem of *naródnost'* by considering it on a socio-historical basis within the framework of the development of class society. By destroying the feudal basis of society, he said, the bourgeoisie also condemned to extinction the art forms associated with it. But the revolutionary element in the exploited class of the new, bourgeois society begins to produce its own, new 'popular' art and it is to this that Marx and Engels turned their attention. They cited, for example, the 'Song of the Weavers'[16] of the Silesian workers. They were not unaware of the limitations of such phenomena but they saw in them evidence of both the ability and the desire of the workers to create their own art. This argument was taken further by Lénin in a number of articles and in the Soviet Union such forms of new 'popular' art are actively encouraged and subsidised.[17]

* However, a socialist society not only preserves the best in folk or 'popular' art; it instils new ideas into them, leading to a fusion of traditional forms with the finest achievements of academic art. Universal education and the consequent raising of the cultural level of the entire people, with improved living standards and ample leisure, will then give rise to the 'new, great Communist art'[18] that Lénin predicted.

3

From even such a brief exposition it becomes clear that *naródnost'* in the arts does not simply pertain to accessibility to the masses in the sense of simplicity of form. Art, if it is to be 'popular', must not only be intelligible to the masses, it must spring from them. The link between the masses and folk art, whether traditional or new, is clear; the link with the 'popular' elements in academic art is more complex. We shall now examine this further by reference to a second major principle of Marxist-Leninist aesthetic theory, the principle of the *klássovost'* – the class nature – of art.

* For most of its history, human society has been divided into classes, and this has led to a clash of ideologies between them. This is inevitably reflected in art, though in complicated and sometimes oblique fashion.

* All great works of art reflect, to some extent, the class ideology of the artists who created them, but this does not mean that they do not contain 'popular' elements. Even folk art reflects class differences; peasant art, for instance, has a different ideological content from proletarian art.* Moreover in a capitalist society the ideology of the ruling class is partly echoed in the art of the masses. (In a socialist society, these elements of ruling-class ideology, 'survivals of capitalism', must be isolated and expunged.) And within the ruling class certain ideological differences may develop, though these are quickly reconciled in the face of a common threat.[19]

* The content of a work of art is not entirely determined by the ideology of the artist himself, since every genuine artist is a reflection to some degree of the reality of his epoch. His subject is life in all its basic aspects, and the major importance of his work lies in its objective content, even though this may be obscured or even contradicted by his own subjective views, dictated by the form of the society in which he works.

* At some stage each rising class, moving towards the status of ruling class, embodies progressive, social-evolutionary tendencies and therefore represents the interests of the majority, including the exploited class. Hence the necessity in every case to determine the concrete historical conditions in which the class nature of any work of art is manifested. In every society, as Lénin indicated, there are two cultures – the culture of the exploiter and the culture of the exploited,[20] So when considering a given epoch it is essential to decide what is reactionary and what is genuinely 'popular', avoiding the errors resulting from the automatic application of 'vulgar sociological' criteria.

* By revealing the immorality of the clergy in the *Decameron*, Boccaccio displayed his opposition to feudalism; by describing his *Utopia*, in which private property did not exist, Thomas More took up an anti-bourgeois position; and by portraying the miserable consequence of an unhappy marriage in *Anna Karénina*, Tolstóy condemned the values of the society of his day. No matter what sphere of human life the artist portrays, he reveals his attitude to society and consequently the ideology of the classes within that society and their relationship with the masses.

* Likewise in the visual arts, in which, as in literature, the choice of subject

* Though Soviet society is said to be classless in the conventional sense, it nevertheless admits of two major classes – the peasants and the industrial proletariat – and a stratum (*proslóika*) of intelligentsia.

or hero may betray class attitudes. This may be explicit, as in Venetsiánov's choice of peasant life as the subject of his painting instead of the traditional portraits of the nobility. Or it may be more subtle: the art and sculpture of the Middle Ages, under the influence of religious faith, emphasised man's spiritual aspect, whereas the masters of Renaissance art – Raphael, Michelangelo, Leonardo da Vinci – aspired to portray the harmony between his spiritual and physical attributes.

4

These examples illustrate the widely different ways in which class attitudes may be seen in works of art. Marxist analysis sets out to show that art has profound social significance even when it has no obvious or direct concern with social problems. In this argument an especially important and difficult question is that of the philosophy (world-view) of the individual artist, for the artist's own philosophy is also inseparable from his art.

* Genuine art cannot flourish on the basis of a false philosophy: underlying all great art are ideals of humanism, belief in life and in man, faith in the capacity of the human mind to comprehend reality, indignation at social evil and a vision of the perfect conditions for the development of the human personality. But if the work of an individual artist betrays conservative or reactionary views, this does not necessarily mean that his entire philosophy is false. Balzac was a legitimist, but this does not detract from his condemnation of bourgeois greed. Similarly Tolstóy's principle of non-violent resistance to evil was misguided but it was not central to his work which, in the main evinced a correct understanding of his times. An artist's philosophy embraces the whole of life and must not be judged on the basis of isolated false or erroneous ideas conditioned by the society in which he lives.

* Marxism reveals that art always bears traces of class interests and has always participated in the class struggle, though this is most clearly visible at times of social upheaval. Thus in the period preceding the French revolution the arts played an important role in ideological preparation for that event and in nineteenth century Russia the poetry of Púshkin, Lérmontov and Nekrásov; the writings of Gógol, Turgénev, Chernyshévsky and Tolstóy; the plays of Ostróvsky; the paintings of Kramskóy, Súrikov and Répin; and the music of Glínka, Chaikóvsky, Borodín, Dargomýzhsky and Rímsky-Kórsakov all played an enormous part in awakening social consciousness and protest. Similarly during the Revolution and Civil War artists took an active part in the struggle – Mayakóvsky with his verse, Demyán Bédny with his satire, and Móor and Dení with their posters. But a scientific application of the principle of *klássovost'* in an examination of ideological matters requires careful study of all aspects if the errors of 'vulgar sociology', already mentioned, are to be avoided.

* They have not always been avoided, and in the early stages of the development of Soviet literary studies certain erroneous ideas gained great

popularity. Attempts were made to relate the progress of art too directly to the technical-economic base of society (e.g. to relate statistics concerning the import–export of corn in the early nineteentth century directly to Púshkin's poetry!), even though Marx had warned against this.[21] The 'popular' quality of artistic works will guarantee their survival long after the society that gave them birth has receded into past history and this contributes to the complex nature of the relationship between art and society.

* A similar error lay at the root of the Proletkult [22] desire to renounce all bourgeois art – all the art of the pre-revolutionary era. The members of this movement did not realise that by renouncing bourgeois art they were cutting themselves off from the genuinely 'popular' elements that it contained.

Lénin's opposition to the Proletkult,[23] which is sometimes presented as merely the Communist Party's opposition to any kind of rivalry, may therefore be seen to have had a deep ideological cause, and this is a valuable lesson in the correct understanding of the meaning of *naródnost'*. We shall return to this topic in our discussion of policy in the 1920s.

* The Proletkult was not alone in vulgarising Marxist principles. Both Engels [24] and Marx [25] had already had occasion to comment on the over-simplification that underlay the tendency to relate artistic and aesthetic phenomena too closely to the economic base of society. The same class phenomenon may acquire different traits, depending on concrete historical conditions. To label a work of art 'bourgeois' and therefore automatically attribute to it all the worst features of the bourgeoisie is a gross over-simplification. Not all writers of the bourgeois period were themselves conscious protagonists of bourgeois ideology, though their horizons were of necessity restricted. Moreover, the bourgeoisie was in its day the most progressive section of society. This theme was also taken up by Lénin;[26] in the 'vulgar sociological' view the artist is a selfish protagonist of his own class interests and embodies this attitude in his art, but to the Marxist-Leninist it is important to define in art, as in social consciousness in general, the degree to which objective reality is consciously reflected. Since art, as a form of social consciousness, is able to reflect objective reality, this quality must be visible in the work of the individual artists. It was in such a context that Lénin could discuss Tolstóy as the mirror of the Russian revolution.[27]

* All genuine art contains an objective reflection of at least some basic aspects of the life of the society of the times, and this is the criterion of its realism and its social significance. The *klássovost'* of a work of art is expressed in the manner, extent and profundity of its conscious reflection of reality, and especially of the contradictions in society. In other words, the social significance of a work of art is directly related to its realism, that is, to its objective reflection of reality.

* By their truthful and broad grasp of reality, depth of penetration into the essence of social relations and accurate depiction of the personal life and experience of individual characters in the context of society as a whole major works of art acquire a 'popular' nature, since accurate depiction of reality is always a spur to progress. The artist may bear the imprint of

class, but by producing an objective reflection of life and the laws that govern its development he creates a work of art that transcends the bounds of class ideology. Though Plekhánov saw Tolstóy as merely a representative of the 'conscience-stricken nobility', Lénin was able to show that the basis of his philosophy was the ideology of the masses of the peasantry. And Dostoyévsky, though in later works such as the novel *Devils* (*Bésy*) a frank proponent of reaction, has nevertheless great social significance because of the depth of his psychological analysis and of the themes and conflicts portrayed in his writing. Concerning such authors as Dostoyévsky the question that must be put is not a dogmatic – 'Was he a "popular" artist or not?', but a dialectic – 'What elements in his work have an essentially "popular" nature?' All artists are conditioned by the class structure of the society in which they live, but by their reflection of objective reality, their realism, their works assume a genuinely 'popular' aspect even though the artists may appear as protagonists of reaction or of illusory solutions to the problems of society.

* All art is class art. The class nature of art is visible even in socialist societies; wherever class antagonisms exist, they are reflected in art. The Soviet Union, being a classless society in the sense of having no class antagonisms within it, is nevertheless almost unique and alone in a predominantly capitalist world, and in such a context all Soviet art is also class art. But Soviet society is monolithic, hence the *naródnost'* and *klássovost'* of Soviet art coincides. And since Soviet society is united behind the Communist Party, the *naródnost'* and *klássovost'* of Soviet art find their expression in *partiinost'* – the third major tenet of Marxist-Leninist aesthetics.

5

The principle of *partiinost'*, perhaps the most individual and certainly the most controversial Leninist gloss on Marxist aesthetics, arouses passions both inside and outside the Soviet Union. In a sense it is the professional, practical revolutionary's logical, if extreme, development of the early Marxist theoretician's principle of tendentiousness in art. Extrapolated from one single article [28] it gives Soviet aesthetics their unique flavour, though it traces its antecedents back, in particular, to the works and activities of the founders of Marxism.

* Discussing the artists of the Renaissance, Engels commented that what was especially characteristic of them was that they nearly all 'participated in the practical struggle, taking one side or another – some fighting with word and pen, some with the sword, some with both . . .'[29] In the same way Milton became the poet of the English bourgeois revolution in the seventeenth century, and in France the 'encyclopaedia' of Diderot and D'Alembert was the focal point around which the ideological battle was fought, David was a Jacobin, Delacroix – by his painting 'Liberty Leading the People' – is in-

separably linked with the revolution of 1830 and Courbet is rightly considered the artist of the Paris Commune.

* Engels called this identification with a political or social cause 'tendentiousness' and saw it most clearly at times of heightened class antagonism.
But the degree of social awareness of such artists was clearly restricted by
their lack of understanding of *klássovost'*; hence a clear distinction must
be drawn between *tendentiousness* – the artist's desire to take up a political
stance, and *partíinost'* – a fully articulated awareness of the political function
of art. These are two closely related concepts, sometimes even indistinguish-
able from one another, but they must not be considered identical.

* The founders of Marxism appreciated the problem of consolidating
artistic forces around the proletarian revolutionary movement and making
the most talented artists conscious partisans of the working class cause,
though they did not see this in terms of allegiance to a political party. Their
task was essentially an educative one, as witnessed by their correspondence
about Herwegh and Freilingrath,[30] their critical analysis of Lasalle's drama
Franz von Sickingen,[31] and Engels's mentorship of Margaret Harkness [32] and
Minna Kautsky. Writing to the last named in Paris in November 1885, on
the subject of her novel *Old Ones and the New*, Engels stated: 'Thus the
socialist problem novel ... fully carries out its mission if by a faithful portrayal of the real relations it dispels the dominant conventional illusions
concerning those relations ... without itself offering a direct solution of the
problem involved ...[33]

* The crucial moment in the evolution of the principle of *partíinost'* was
the publication in Górky's journal *Novaya Zhizn'* (*The New Life*) of Lénin's
article on 'Party Organisation and Party Literature' in 1905, at a time when
publication of the party 'press' had become legal for the first time. This
article is of fundamental importance to an understanding of subsequent
developments, for despite allegations that it was dictated simply by the temporary political requirements of the times, it has in fact been vitally influential in determining party policy toward the arts ever since it first
appeared.[34]

* 'Emerging from the captivity of feudal censorship', Lénin wrote, 'we
have no desire to become, and we shall not become, prisoners of bourgeois-
-shopkeeper literary relations.' Then follows one of the most significant statements: 'We want to establish, and we shall establish, a free press, free not
simply from the police, but also from capital, from careerism and, what is
more, free from bourgeois-anarchist individualism.'

* This definition of freedom is central to Lénin's argument, for the freedom of the artist as he envisaged it is vastly different from the 'bourgeois
freedom' he attacked. In a bourgeois society, art serves only the 'upper ten
thousand', and this in itself imposes obvious limitations on the freedom of the
artist. Bourgeois freedom is in fact illusory, depending ultimately on the
purse. Art may be genuinely free only when it is released from all hindrance
in the fulfilment of its true social function, which is to serve the interests of
the masses, 'the millions and tens of millions of working people – the flower
of the country, its strength and its future'. Thus Lénin relates the freedom of
the arts to their *naródnost'*, contrasting the 'hypocritically free literature,

which is in reality linked with the bourgeoisie, with a really free one that will be *openly* linked with the proletariat'. It will be free because it will not feed on 'greed or careerism' but on 'the idea of socialism and sympathy with the working people', serving the interests of the masses and enriching revolutionary thought with the practical experience of the socialist proletariat. 'In this way it will bring about a 'permanent interaction between the experience of the past (scientific socialism . . .) and the experience of the present . . .'

* The essence of *partiinost'* is the open allegiance of art to the cause of the working class, a conscious decision on the part of the artist to dedicate his work to the furtherance of socialism. It is not inimicable to freedom; on the contrary, it affords the artist the optimum conditions for the development of his ideological aspirations, guaranteeing him an organic link with the people and a place within its ranks. Literature therefore becomes '*part* of the common cause of the proletariat', part of 'one single, great Social-Democratic mechanism set in motion by the entire politically-conscious vanguard of the entire working class'. It becomes an organic element in the struggle for socialism and an active weapon in that process.

* From this it follows that Party guidance is essential if art is to escape from 'bourgeois-anarchic individualism', with its damaging effect on the relationship between the artist and the masses and hence on art itself. The 'organised socialist proletariat' must supervise it from beginning to end and 'infuse into it the life-stream of the living proletarian cause', putting an end to the traditional situation in which 'the writer does the writing, the reader does the reading'. The reader must have a hand in the writing, too.

* Lénin acknowledges that literature lends itself least of all to 'mechanical adjustment or levelling', and that 'in this field greater scope must undoubtedly be allowed for personal initiative, individual inclination, thought and fantasy, form and content'. But all this means is that allowance must be made for the specific features of literature in a purely technical sense: 'This, however, does not in the least refute the proposition, alien and strange to the bourgeoisie and bourgeois democracy, that literature must . . . become an element of Social-Democratic work, inseparably bound up with the other elements.'

* * *

From such a source the principle of *partiinost'* has evolved into the most important, single guiding factor in Soviet policy toward the arts, providing the unifying element that draws together the several strands in Marxist-Leninist aesthetics that we have examined. It embodies, or 'demands from the artist', a threefold, conscious decision: (1) art must fulfil a specific social function; (2) that function is to further the interests of the masses; (3) to further the interests of the masses, art must become part of the activity of the Communist Party.

Although the argument continues about what precisely Lénin meant in his article – it raged particularly fiercely inside the Soviet Union during the period following Stálin's death – there is no doubt of the importance attached to that article, and its interpretation, in present-day Soviet aesthetics : 'Exclusion of the principle of *partiinost'* not only impoverishes the principle but gives grounds to our ideological enemies for placing a distorted interpretation on it – grounds of which they frequently take advantage.' [35]

In the introduction to this book it was pointed out that one of the most outstanding Soviet writers, Mikhaíl Shólokhov, is often quoted by Western commentators as having been unable to explain what Socialist Realism is. On the other hand, Soviet critics would themselves quote a passage from Shólokhov's speech at the Second Writers' Congress (1954) on the subject of *partiinost'* : 'Our furious enemies in other countries say that we Soviet authors write according to the dictates of the Party. But the fact of the matter is a little different. Each of us writes according to the dictates of his heart, but all our hearts belong to the Party and to the people, whom we serve with our art.' [36]

Socialist Realism, it must be stressed in conclusion, is the 'artistic method' whereby the artist fulfils the demands put upon him by the Communist Party. It should therefore be carefully distinguished from that *social realism* which, in the parlance of Western critics, may be taken to refer to the artist's concern with social themes, not with a political programme. In a Russian context such social realism was very much a nineteenth century phenomenon, whereas Socialist Realism is a twentieth century development. The relationship between the two is the theme of our second chapter.

2 Art and the Party

> ... He would not attack the book at once, he would start with some
> sacrosanct pronouncement by Belinsky or Nekrasov – something that
> only the blackest villain could quarrel with – and he would subtly
> twist their words, give them a meaning they were never intended to
> have – and very soon he would show, with Belinsky or Herzen as
> his witness, that Galakhov's new book showed his vicious, anti-
> social character and revealed the shaky foundations of his philosophy.
>
> Solzhenitsyn: *The First Circle*

PRECISELY how justified are contemporary Soviet theoreticians in
interpreting Lénin's article on 'Party Organisation and Party Literature' [1]
as they do is a question which is the subject of constant debate. They are
certainly rather touchy on the subject themselves, adopting a plainly
defensive attitude in many of their statements: 'V. I. Lenin's article ... is
a theoretical document that has a fundamental significance for the entire
period of the socialist revolution and the building of communism. *This
must be stressed with all possible force*, since there have been attempts on
the part of revisionists to assert that this work was evoked only by the
political demands of the moment – the revolution of 1905 – and referred
only to the conditions of the time ...' [2]

The use of the term 'revisionists' is significant here; the defence is
against not only bourgeois attacks – which are to be expected – but attacks
by fellow socialists.

Both kinds of critic reject the authority of the 1905 article, on two
counts: firstly, because Lénin's propositions have no precedent in Marx
and Engels (we have already pointed out the essential difference between
tendentiousness and *partiinost'*); and secondly, because the article clearly
referred to party literature only, and this in the sense of the press, meaning newspapers and journals. They cite a passage from the article that
Soviet commentators more often prefer to ignore:

> ... What! some intellectual, an ardent champion of liberty, may shout.
> What, you want to impose collective control on such a delicate, indi-
> vidual matter as literary work! You want workmen to decide questions

of science, philosophy, or aesthetics by a majority of votes! You deny
the absolute freedom of absolutely individual ideological work!

Calm yourselves, gentlemen! First of all, we are discussing party
literature and its subordination to party control. Everyone is free to
write and say whatever he likes, without any restrictions...[3]

Support for such a point of view is also adduced from the comments of
Nadézhda Krúpskaya, Lénin's widow.[4]

For the student of the arts in the Soviet Union the question of what
precisely Lénin did mean is of less importance than the use to which
his statements have been put. Our object in this study is not to pass judgements on Soviet policy or to criticise the premises on which that policy
is based, so much as to reveal precisely what the policy is and how it was
formulated. On the other hand we can fully understand neither the policy
nor the practice without a further examination of Lénin's thinking in
related fields, especially as he devoted comparatively little of his writing
to a discussion of the arts as such at least in a conventional sense. For the
basic question, surely, is not whether in 1905 Lénin had in mind only
the Social Democratic press, but whether – if he had – this would in-
validate his propositions for application in the changed circumstances that
followed the successful assumption of power by the Bolsheviks in 1917. If
in 1905 he had in mind only the Social-Democratic press, can his propositions not logically be applied to the whole of the press in a situation in
which that party – in a new guise – is the only party? Similarly in a situation in which the arts are assigned a specific social function defined in
terms of support for a political programme, are we not, in attempting to
divorce literature from other forms of writing, imposing a distinction
without a difference? We may gain some useful insight into Lénin's
thinking by an examination of his periodisation of the Russian revolutionary movement, but first let us look briefly at his attitude to the
sanctity of Marx's writings, in reply to the 'revisionist's' allegation that
the propositions embodied in – or extrapolated from – the 1905 article
have no precedent in Marx.

I

'We stand entirely on the ground of Marxist theory',[5] Lénin wrote at
the turn of the century, but he would certainly have echoed Plekhánov's
view that the ideas and aspirations of the Russian Social Democrats were
an organic development of the previous history of the Russian revolutionary movement.[6] In fact, he made this explicit in a number of his later

writings, in which his constant theme was the necessity to define and take due account of the specific peculiarities of the Russian situation in order to work out the correct organisation and policy for the Russian Social Democratic party. The raw material that had to be sifted was the history of socialism and democracy in the West, as well as the history and experience of the revolutionary movement in Russia, but 'the actual "working-out" of the material must be independent, for there is nowhere for us to find ready-made models...' [7] In reply to the literalists and vulgarisers he asserted that imitation and borrowing were legitimate only when the precise problems in Russia were the same as those elsewhere, 'but in no circumstances must they lead to a neglect of the *peculiarities* of the Russian situation...' [8] In fact, on various topics Lénin looked upon Marx's writings as essentially raw material that must be developed on Russian soil to meet the precise demands of the specifically Russian dilemma: 'We certainly do not consider Marx's theory complete and inviolable; on the contrary, we are convinced that it provides only the cornerstone for the science that socialists *must* push further in all directions, if they do not wish to lose contact with reality...' [9]

In this context we might do well to point out that Lénin's own 'theory', too, was neither 'complete' nor 'inviolable'. He certainly had no detailed plan of action for each situation or field of activity, and the arts is perhaps one such field. Yet it is the development of Lénin's theory that forms the basis of current policy, which is the object of our present interest.

2

What, then, was Lénin's periodisation of the Russian revolutionary movement, and how does its interpretation contribute to our understanding of Soviet policy toward the arts and, in particular, of Socialist Realism?

Lénin's development of Marxist theory involved both taking it a stage further and combining it with the native Russian tradition, while nevertheless not attempting to update ideas evolved at an earlier period. Even ideas evolved in the nineteenth century in the light of the specific Russian situation could not simply be mechanically applied in the twentieth century, especially after the great turning point of the 1905 Revolution. Nevertheless the twentieth century theories were evolved, at least in part, from those of the great nineteenth century thinkers – Hérzen, Belínsky, Chernyshévsky, Dobrolyúbov and the rest – whom Lénin investigated deeply before producing his analysis into three stages: 'The emancipation movement in Russia has passed through three main stages, corresponding to the three main classes of Russian society, which have left their impress on the movement: (1) the period of the nobility, roughly from 1825 to 1861; (2) the *raznochíntsy* or bourgeois-democratic period, approximately from 1861 to 1895; and (3) the proletarian period, from 1895 to the present time.' [10]

The first period does not include Radíshchev, except obliquely through the influence of his 'Journey from St Petersburg to Moscow' on the revolutionary nobility of that period, the Decembrists. However, that influence is said to have been so great that in this sense, Radíshchev, too, belongs to the nineteenth-century movement. This centred on the Decembrists, though it was not confined simply to those who actually took part in their uprising in 1825. Púshkin, for example, was very much a sympathiser with their views; hence the *naródnost'* of his poetry, which not only enriched itself, as we have seen, from folk traditions, but represented, from the Marxist-Leninist standpoint, the aspirations of the masses.

An attempt to analyse the Decembrist revolt from this aspect was made by Plekhánov in 1900,[11] though not from the point of view of *klássovost'*. Plekhánov established the continuity of the revolutionary movement begun by the Decembrists, and this argument was developed much further by Lénin, who acknowledged the great influence they had exerted on him personally. In *What is to be Done?* he related how the 'elders' of the St Petersburg Social Democrats, of whom he was one, were jokingly called 'Decembrists'.[12]

Lénin admired the Decembrists for the fact that they had risen in arms against the Tsar, championing the republican cause and calling for an end to the feudal system of serf-law. In his testament to Hérzen, however, he defines their major service to the revolutionary cause: 'These revolutionaries formed but a narrow group. They were terribly far removed from the people. But their efforts were not in vain. The Decembrists awakened Hérzen, and Hérzen began the work of revolutionary agitation.' [13]

In fact, it is to Hérzen that Lénin devoted most of his discussion of the first period, though his enthusiasm was well counter-balanced by sober criticism. Hérzen 'rose to a height which placed him on a level with the greatest thinkers of his time. He assimilated Hegel's dialectics . . . came right up to dialectical materialism, and halted . . . before historical materialism.' Hence his merits – and his defects, the 'spiritual shipwreck' he suffered after the defeat of the 1848 revolution. At that time he was a revolutionary, a democrat, even a socialist, but his socialism was that of the petty-bourgeois : 'In point of fact, it was not socialism at all, but so many sentimental phrases, benevolent visions, which were the expression *at that time* of the revolutionary character of the bourgeois democrats, as well as of the proletariat, which had not yet freed itself from the influence of those democrats.' [14]

3

The second period of the revolutionary movement dates from the 1860s, after the emancipation of the serfs and the disillusion that followed it. The mental revolution experienced by the Russian intelligentsia in the sixties, Lénin agreed, was as great as that experienced by the French intelligentsia in the second half of the eighteenth century.[15] The period was marked by a change of leadership in the revolutionary movement, from the nobility to the *raznochíntsy*, and the rise of a culture that was reflected in literature and criticism, journalism, pedagogy, the arts and the sciences. The vanguard was now the classless intelligentsia 'who belonged not to the nobility but to the civil servants, urban petty bourgeois, merchant and peasant classes,' [16] and their forerunner, even before the emancipation of the serfs in 1861, was Belínsky, whose influence was paramount. Though the socialism of the Petrashévsky circle was utopian, not scientific, Lénin nevertheless considered that 'the embryo of the populist movement (*naródnichestvo*) was conceived not in the 1860s but in the 1840s',[17] and this he attributed to Belínsky.

Questioning the traditional analysis of the Slavophil/Westerner controversy, Lénin saw Belínsky's great contribution as the polarisation of the Westerners into liberal reformers, on the one hand, and revolutionaries, on the other. In particular, Belínsky's attitude to the role of art in the social debate was very much to Lénin's taste. 'In our times art and literature have become more than ever before an expression of social questions', Belínsky had stated approvingly in his article 'On the Russian Literature of 1847', and in Lénin's opinion his 'Letter to Gógol' had been one of the best things published in the uncensored democratic press, which 'preserves an enormous and active interest to this very day.' [18] In his attack on the anthology *Vékhi* (*Landmarks*), which defined Belínsky's letter as 'a lurid and classic expression of intellectual sentiment' and which he dubbed 'an encyclopaedia of liberal renegacy', Lénin defended Belínsky as a publicist against the charge of expressing, with Chernyshévsky and Dobrolyúbov, 'only a mood of the intelligentsia, rather than a genuine, democratic motif'.[19] And in *What is to be Done?* he related the role of the classless intelligentsia with his concept of the role of the Party, further developed in the article of 1905: '... *the role of the vanguard fighter can be fulfilled only by a party which is guided by the advanced theory*.[20] In order to understand what this means at all clearly, let the reader recall the predecessors of Russian Social-Democracy, like Hérzen, Belínsky, Chernyshévsky and the brilliant galaxy of the revolutionaries of the seventies.' [21]

In claiming a direct line of descent from the Russian thinkers of the nineteenth century, the Marxist-Leninist does not, of course, imply that his forebears were not themselves influenced by ideas imported from the West. Various commentators, notably Isaiah Berlin, have remarked how seedlings imported from Western Europe run riot when transplanted in Russian soil, acquiring a mutant nature unknown to their originators. It was above all from the French revolution that the Decembrists had received their inspiration, though their own background necessarily made them somewhat selective in their choice of models. Few of them approved of the Committee of Public Safety, and whereas they extolled the virtues of Lafayette and Mirabeau, they were horrified by Robespierre and Marat. And it is of particular interest to English readers to recall that one of the Decembrists, N. I. Turgénev, travelled to England to become acquainted at first hand with Robert Owen's New Lanark experiment. There was an already long-established tradition of russification of Western ideas when Lénin thought it necessary to warn of the dangers of slavish imitation.[22]

It seems indisputable that Hérzen and Belínsky were acquainted with Marx's early works, but contemporary Soviet scholars see not so much the influence of Marx as a parallel development of thought.[23] They point to striking resemblances, for instance, between Belínsky's criticism of Eugène Sue's *Mystères de Paris* and Marx's own assessment of that novel, while commenting that 'as yet there are no works elucidating the unquestionable similarities and major differences between the ideological evolution of Marx and Engels, on the one hand, and Belínsky and Hérzen, on the other.' [24] Even so, in his analysis of the Russian nineteenth century revolutionary movement, Lénin moves significantly in this direction, and in his own writing he was himself a bridge between the two.

Whatever his attitude to Belínsky and Hérzen, there is ample evidence that closest to Lénin's heart amongst the forerunners of Russian Marxism was undoubtedly Chernyshévsky, whose novel *What is to be Done?* (a title subsequently to be used by Lénin) inspired him from his early student days. Lénin's literary taste is interestingly illuminated by his reaction to this novel: 'Now this is real literature! It teaches, guides and inspires!' [25]

His admiration of Chernyshévsky found expression in a whole series of works, as well as in his comments on monographs by Plekhánov and Steklóv. Attacking the liberal populists (naródniķi), who claimed descent from Hérzen and Chernyshévsky, Lénin stressed the latter's true revolutionary credo, distorted by the liberals,[26] and pointed out the depth of Chernyshévsky's conscious understanding of his times. 'At a time when the peasant reforms were only just being introduced, it took the genius of Chernyshévsky to realise so clearly their basically bourgeois nature.'[27] He abominated the reforms, willing them to fail, so that the government's tightrope act between the landowners and liberals would collapse and an open class-struggle develop. He represented the revolutionary democratic wing, whose opposition to the liberal reformers gathered strength throughout the entire second period and continued into the third.

Lénin characterised Chernyshévsky as being both utopian socialist and revolutionary democrat, and admired him above all for his merciless criticism of liberal hypocrisy. 'Chernyshévsky infected Lénin with his irreconcilable hostility to the liberals',[28] and in this attitude Lénin never wavered. It was here, as in his assessment of Chernyshévsky's own attitude, that he parted company at the turn of the century with Plekhánov. But he was equally opposed to attempts to tone down the utopian nature of Chernyshévsky's socialism or to claim that he was a Marxist. Chernyshévsky was a utopian socialist who wished to achieve socialism via the semi-feudal peasant commune, being unable to see that only capitalism and the proletariat could create the necessary material base. But he was also a revolutionary democrat who, in circumstances of extreme disadvantage, was nevertheless able to influence political affairs towards a mass struggle of the peasantry against the established order.[29]

The progressive thinkers of the 1840s–60s, who wished to see the development of European 'scientific' civilisation in Russia, were in subsequent polemics referred to as the 'enlighteners', and the Marxists as the 'disciples'. Foremost amongst the 'enlighteners' of the sixties were Chernyshévsky and Dobrolyúbov, both of whom Engels labelled 'Russian socialist Lessings'.[30] In his reply[31] to Mikhailóvsky's attack on the Marxists in 1897,[32] Lénin made a clear statement of the quarrel with the Populists in the context of each group's attitude to these 'enlighteners'.

The 'enlighteners' approved of the course of developments in society, because they were unable to see its inherent contradictions; the Populists saw those contradictions and therefore feared the development; and the 'disciples' saw their hope for the future only in the deepening of the contradictions, and therefore also approved of the development. Thus the 'enlighteners' and the 'disciples' wished to speed the development, and the Populists to retard it. The outlook of 'enlighteners' and 'disciples' was optimistic, but whereas the former concentrated on overcoming the vestiges of the past order, without posing questions about the future, the latter wished to speed the development of capitalism and, with it, of a revolutionary proletariat. To the Populists, whose outlook was pessimistic, capitalism was reactionary. Thus the true heirs of the 'enlighteners' were the Marxists, and not the Populists, and the line of descent was established from Chernyshévsky and Dobrolyúbov to Lénin.

4

This applied equally in the field of aesthetics; indeed, in Chernyshévsky's aesthetic theory, and in the novel *What is to be Done?* as exemplification of that theory in practice, we seem to have the most important formative factors in Lénin's own attitudes to aesthetics, literature and the arts.[33] And in such a context the task of interpreting Lénin's article of 1905 becomes rather less difficult and perhaps somewhat less controversial than it might have seemed.

Applying Feuerbach's views to the arts, though prevented by the censor from mentioning that dangerous name explicitly, Chernyshévsky posed the basic propositions of his materialist aesthetics in his thesis 'the Aesthetic Relations of Art and Reality', presented at the University of St Petersburg in 1855 and subsequently developed further. The artist, he declared, could not and must not limit himself to depicting the beautiful aspects of reality – love, youth, true friendship, heroism, nobility, etc. 'Art does not limit itself only to the beautiful. . . . It embraces the whole of reality. . . . The content of art is the social aspect of life. . . .' If this is so, then by such content art draws closer to life, it becomes concerned with more 'real' themes, and it dedicates itself to the service of man. Art must provide a true reflection of reality, interpreting that reality and judging it, so that reality itself may be reshaped. Reality is always superior to art; the highest function of art is to be a 'textbook of life'. The artist must react to the problems of the day, explaining their essence and pointing the way to their solution, though his ideas must not remain as abstract theories; they must be embodied in images and events. . . . Art, then, has a definite social and didactic role; the first seeds of Socialist Realism are sown.

In his discussion of the basic question of aesthetics – the nature of beauty – Chernyshévsky seems to foreshadow subsequent statements concerning the 'typical', which in socialist-realist parlance implies not what is most representative of what is but a model – elaborated from the best features of the present – of what will be in the Communist society of the future.[34] Dismissing the idealists' argument Chernyshévsky propounds a simple definition 'Beauty is life'. This he amplifies significantly: 'The beautiful is that in which we can see life as it ought, in our understanding, to be ...' And though not a Marxist and not arguing in terms of class, he came close to the concept of *klássovost* – as this is now understood – in discussing the influence of social background on the concept of the beautiful; hence the educative function of art, which must – as Lénin said that Chernyshévsky's own novel did – teach, guide and inspire. The relationship in this sphere between Chernyshévsky and Lénin was perhaps best stated by Lunachársky: 'Vladímir Ilyích considered that art must be 'popular', that it must elevate the masses, teach them and strengthen them. In this respect Vladímir Ilyích was a direct descendant of Chernyshévsky.'[35]

On only a few occasions did Lénin single out Dobrolyúbov – whose name is naturally coupled with that of Chernyshévsky – for special, individual mention, preferring to consider him as a disciple, though not a mere imitator, of 'that really great Russian writer'[36] who, from the point of view of philosophy and aesthetics, stood sometimes a little way behind Engels, sometimes on a par with him.[37] In both he admired their burning enmity toward the serf system and all its consequences, staunch advocacy of 'enlightenment' and the development in Russia of a society based on Western European science, and selfless support for the peasant masses.[38] Such were the attitudes to which the 'disciples' were proud to proclaim themselves heirs, reinforcing them and reworking them in the light of Marxist theory. Appraising Dobrolyúbov's critical essays on Goncharóv's novel *Oblómov* and Turgénev's *On the Eve* (*Nakanúne*), Lénin saw them as clarion calls to revolution, and with the journal *Dawn* (*Zaryá*) in mind he exclaimed: 'That's just the sort of literary criticism we need!'[39] This in itself is amply illustrative of Lénin's attitude to the role of the literary critic, and the width of the gulf that separated him from the protagonists of elitist art.[40]

Nekrásov's publication in *Sovreménnik* (*The Contemporary*) in 1860 of Dobrolyúbov's article on *Nakanúne*, 'Oh when will the real day come?' (*Kogdá zhe pridët nastoyáshchii den'*) had precipitated the open rift between liberal reformers and revolutionaries, the polarisation of which Lénin attributed to Belínsky. First Turgénev, then Tolstóy, Goncharóv and Grigoróvich left the journal, predicting its imminent closure, though in fact it continued till 1866 as the platform of Chernyshévsky, Dobrol-yúbov, Nekrásov and Saltykóv-Shchedrín. It is obvious that the rift between the two groups pertained not only to politics but also to the nature and function of the art they all professed. We have seen how Chernyshévsky defined these; let us look briefly at the other members of this group.

Dobrolyúbov, in fact, survived the split by one year only, dying in 1861 at the age of twenty-five, yet having achieved enough in this short span to be placed by Engels on a level with Diderot and Lessing.[41] In essence he continued the tradition of Belínsky: the artist must be close to the masses, able to comprehend their interests and their needs. 'The measure of the worth of a writer or work of art,' he wrote, 'we take to be the extent to which they serve as expressions of the natural aspirations of the given epoch or people.' [42] Art must serve the people: 'We shall never agree that a poet who wastes his talent on model depictions of leaves or brooks can be of equal stature with one who, with the same degree of talent, can reproduce, for instance, some phenomenon of social life.' Art must not only reflect life, it must pronounce judgements on it, he echoed Chernyshévsky, and 'the greatest merit of the writer-artist is in the truth of his depiction. . . .' The attitude of the artist to reality is reflected in that of the critic to a work of art . . . 'he studies it, trying to define its own norm, to assemble its basic, characteristic traits'. The real meaning of a work of art is sometimes not apparent to the artist who created it; in such cases the function of criticism is 'to unravel the idea concealed in the artist's creation'. All these arguments were to be heard afresh in the liter-ary debates of the 1920s.

The year following the death of Dobrolyúbov was to see the almost simultaneous arrest of Chernyshévsky and Písarev – the latter himself to die at twenty-seven, having spent almost five years of his short life in prison. Russian Word (Rússkoye slóvo) in which he published his articles until its closure, with Sovreménnik, in 1866, in many ways complemented the latter journal, and though Písarev differed from Chernyshévsky and Dobrolyúbov in coming of a wealthy, noble family, his antipathy for the social system was violent, and despite his main preoccupation with the popularisation of science in order to solve once and for all 'the inescap-able problem of the hungry and the ragged',[43] his views on art were in some ways similar to those of his contemporaries. Art must serve the broad masses, first of all by disseminating progressive ideas. 'Literature can bring benefit only via new ideas; this is its true function, and in this connection it has no rivals.' But in so far as art detracted from the major problem – that of 'the study and dissemination of the natural sciences' – then art was harmful and always had been. In this sense even Púshkin was nothing but a skilled rhymester, deaf to the needs of the people.

To Lénin, the most appealing aspect of Písarev's thinking was his idea of the inspiring vision that would 'support and strengthen the energy of the working man'. The gulf between reality and vision will cause no harm provided the dreamer really believes in his vision, looks closely at reality, 'and then compares his observations with his castles in the air and works conscientiously to turn his fantasy into fact. When there is a point of contact between dream and life, then everything is for the best.' In so far as such vision gave rise to bold, positive activity, Lénin thought it absurd to deny its value. 'Unfortunately we have too little of such dreaming in our movement', was his comment.[44] And it is not too far a cry to see in Písarev's ideas the germ of that 'revolutionary romanticism' that was later to capture Górky's imagination and to find its way also into Socialist Realism.

Commenting on the early Mayakóvsky's futuristic verses, Lénin remarked that having been 'brought up on Nekrásov' he did not understand the modernistic trends.[45] This is an interesting confirmation of contemporary accounts – even by such avowed enemies as Grigóriyev – that not even Púshkin or Lérmontov had so captured the thoughts and hopes of the people and made such an impact on a whole generation as had Nekrásov. Here we have *naródnost'* in both senses; so precisely did Nekrásov catch the folk idiom that many of his verses instantly became folk songs and remain so to this day. But this is not all: subscribing entirely to Chernyshévsky's aesthetic, Nekrásov revealed the essence of social relations in Tsarist Russia, pinpointing the evils and condemning them. The simplicity and vividness of his deliberately non-'poetic' diction, making his poetry immediately accessible to a wide readership, combined with the 'objectivity' of his depiction of 'reality' (with the exception of subsequently bitterly repented attempts to placate Muravyëv and thus save *Sovreménnik* from closure) and his determination that art should serve the masses, not the elite few, make Nekrásov a model for the proletarian poet.

Ironically it is above all on Mayakóvsky, whom Lénin contrasted with Nekrásov to the severe disadvantage of the former, that the present day Soviet critic detects the older poet's influence. For each an open – indeed, loudly proclaimed – concern with burning social and hence political issues tended to invite either praise or rancour in proportion to the reader's attitude to the issues themselves, that is, in response simply to the content.

But each in his own way evolved poetic forms appropriate to the content, though for Nekrásov this was largely overlooked during his lifetime, and for Mayakóvsky attention to the more obvious innovations of form has sometimes led to a neglect of balanced evaluation of their relationship with that content.

It is certainly beyond doubt that Nekrásov more than any other poet moulded Lénin's appreciation of verse. 'He loved Nekrásov and had a magnificent knowledge of him,' Krúpskaya commented. 'He had almost learned Nekrásov by heart.' [46]

If, to this brilliant gallery of 'men of the sixties' we add another of Lénin's favourite authors, Saltykóv-Shchedrín, whose literary stature is perhaps less controversial and whose viciously portrayed Iúdushka in *The Golovlëvs* (*Gospodá Golovlëvy*) is one of the most memorable characters in the whole of nineteenth century Russian prose – we already have emerging a quite clear picture of Lénin's literary tastes, both in the sense of the function he defined for art and from the point of view of his appreciation of more narrowly 'literary', technical mastery. We must, of course, not commit the 'vulgar' error of assuming that any of these figures were Marxists or that Lénin considered them to be such. They were bourgeois democrats and their outlook, from Lénin's point of view, was therefore severely limited. But each of them, consciously or otherwise, contributed to the evolution of the role that art, and in particular literature, was to play in the later, proletarian period of the revolutionary movement.

In a direct – if apparently paradoxical way – this all accounts for the modern assessment of the *naródnost'* of Górky, whose artistic talent is plain, whose influence at the turn of the century and thereafter was immense, but who, as his embarrassingly naïve speech at the first Writers' Congress testifies, was an ideological infant for whom *partiinost'*, if it did not already exist, had most assuredly to be invented!

5

Considering the 1870s, the Marxists disapproved, as we have seen, of the apolitical and utopian aspects of the Populists' attitudes, even though these traced their origin to Chernyshévsky and, beyond him, to Hérzen. The whole idea of the development of socialism without the intermediate stage of capitalism was absurd; but capitalism could take more than one form, and Lénin was able to approve of the progressive 'historical content' of populism as representing petty bourgeois capitalism, as opposed to the liberal-landowner variety.

Analysing the philosophy of the Populists, Lénin isolated a number of partly conflicting component streams, in particular those whose prime ideologists were Bakúnin, Lavróv and Tkachëv. His assessments of them are of particular interest to our theme.

Bakúnin, like Proudhon, Lasalle and the British trade-unionists was a non-proletarian, non-Marxist socialist and, like Proudhon, an anarchist. But anarchism was a policy of despair, implying a lack of understanding of the class struggle and neglecting the vital need for *education* of the masses. It was the policy of 'the intellectual shaken out of his rut, or of the tramp, but not of the proletariat.' [47] As Lénin was later to point out, it in fact made very little impact on the majority of the people. The anarchists had learned nothing from the fate of the Paris Commune, whereas the Marxists appreciated the need for a long, slow process of education of the masses for revolution.[48] However, anarchism – as one of the most influential factors in the populism of the seventies – had played an important role in the development of the revolutionary movement amongst the peasants. This was especially true of the Land and Will (*Zemlyá i vólya*) faction in the second half of the decade.

Lavróv, on the other hand, was aware that neither the masses nor the intelligentsia were yet ready for revolution and that a massive, socialist *propaganda* programme was required. However, his attempts were badly executed and actually repelled a section of the youth at whom they were directed. And like Bakúnin, Lavróv tended to dissociate politics from economics – hence Lénin's accusation of being apolitical applied to both. Lavróv's *Historical Letters* (*Istorícheskiye pís'ma*), in which he outlined the intelligentsia's duty toward the peasantry, exerted an enormous influence for good, but this did not justify others of Lavróv's ideas, especially his exaggerated estimate of the overall role of the intelligentsia in the socialist revolution. Lavróv and Mikhailóvsky had taken a step backward from Chernyshévsky – from materialism towards positivism.

The unacceptable attitudes which Lénin ascribed to Lavróv were even more typical of Tkachëv and his *nabatists* – so called after their journal *Nabát* (*Alarm Bell*), published abroad. Believing that the established powers in Russia had no class supporting them and were therefore 'hanging in mid-air',[49] Tkachëv saw the coming revolution as a seizure of power by a minority. To the Marxists on the other hand, the problem was not the organisation of conspiracy but the raising up of the proletariat in organised and disciplined fashion via political *agitation*. Only with massive support from the entire proletariat could the revolution be successful.

All these components of populism played a positive role in the development of the revolutionary movement amongst the peasantry and 'rural proletariat', but in essence they were all bourgeois and represented forces with which the Bolsheviks were to clash violently in the twentieth century. However, they were themselves to evolve and shift their groupings throughout the last two decades of the nineteenth century. Thus a split in *Zemlyá i Vólya* in 1879 led to the formation of two groups – The People's Will (*Naródnaya Vólya*) and The Black Partition (*Chërny peredél*), which was to evolve quickly toward Marxism and to lay the first foundation of the Social Democratic movement.

The cause of the failure of the mass 'going to the people' of the mid-seventies – from the Marxist point of view – is stated baldly in the History of CPSU (b): 'The Russian populists wrongly considered that the main revolutionary force was not the working class but the peasantry, and that the power of the Tsar and the land-owners could be overthrown simply by peasant 'revolts'. The populists did not know the working class and did not realise that without uniting with the working class, and without its leadership, the peasants alone would not be able to defeat tsarism and the landowners.' [50]

But the essence of Lénin's approach to the development of the revolutionary movement, and its importance for us, is that he saw its organic, continuing nature, and this applied as much in the arts as in ideology and politics.

6

In literature, painting and music, no less than in criticism and journalism, the 60s and 70s saw the blossoming of the new, bourgeois culture of the *raznochíntsy*. Goncharóv, Turgénev, Tolstóy, Dostoyévsky, Ostróvsky – the liberal writers – became figures of world stature; lesser but yet important writers such as Pomyalóvsky and Reshétnikov began to group themselves around Nekrásov and the journals; but perhaps the most obvious and immediate of Chernyshévsky's disciples were the painters. Though Venetsiánov and Fedótov had shown the way, painting was still 'academic' and far removed from the masses until the group of young artists, many of humble origin, who subsequently became known as *peredvízhniki* [51] began to look to the life of the people for their subjects and inspiration. In the words of Répin, perhaps their foremost exponent, they set out to serve the loftiest aspects of life...' and to criticise mercilessly all the monstrosities of our vile reality'.[52] The challenge to the Academy was first seen in canvasses by Peróv, Myasoyédov, Yákobi and

Púkirev – and the establishment critics, like Ramazánov, were not slow to react: 'Everything has now become infected with tendentiousness; it is all done according to some new recipe prescribed by the Petersburg journals. One has to regret that mature artists waste themselves on such banalities. Surely it would be better for a painter to labour in the name of pure art and to forsake the false path of tendentiousness ... What Peróv produces is not so much a picture as a tendency, a protest ... [53]

With Kramskóy, Répin (*see* Plate II) Savítsky, Shíshkin and the rest, the *peredvízhniki* did for painting what Nekrásov did for poetry and, indeed, their themes were often identical. Like the critics we have already discussed, they were not Marxists and from a Marxist-Leninist point of view they were therefore severely restricted in their understanding of the society of the times, but their *naródnost'* is obvious and the kinship the socialist-realist artist feels with them is demonstrably based on something rather more than the arbitrary stroke of a politician's pen.

In music as in painting the new realism took its aesthetic inspiration from Chernyshévsky, and the *peredvízhniki* had something of a parallel in the *mogúchaya kúchka*, the 'mighty group'. As Fedótov had followed on Venetsiánov, so Dargomýzhsky followed on Glínka, and each was harshly criticised while nevertheless becoming forerunner of a significant trend. But Dargomýzhsky, unlike Fedótov, lived to find himself the centre of a group of talented, if only partly trained, followers. Balákirev, Kuí, Músorgsky, Rímsky-Kórsakov, Borodín – in a society still hypnotised by things foreign, they quickly found themselves labelled 'a nest of ignorant self-advertisers' perpetrating 'musical mutilation'. But they took their music to the public, via their Free Music School, just as the *peredvízhniki* brought their pictures to them in their travelling exhibitions. Like the painters, the musicians sought their subjects in the life of Russia, past and present, and in its literature – Snegúrochka, Sadkó, Borís Godunóv, Khovánshchina, Prince Igor ... Their *naródnost'* was close to Nekrásov's, especially that of Músorgsky, who might well have been speaking for the entire group when he echoed Chernyshévsky in defining the purpose of his art: 'Artistic depiction of beauty alone is grossly infantile, childhood art ... You cannot get by with just pretty sounds. That is not what the modern man wants from art, nor does it justify the artist's efforts. Life, wherever it manifests itself; truth, however bitter; boldness, sincere speaking ... that's my taste, that's what I want.' [54]

Throughout the seventies the reflection of populism is visible in the flourishing of the arts. Though the journal *Sovreménnik* had been closed in 1866, the policies of Chernyshévsky and Dobrolyúbov were continued in *Notes of the Fatherland* (*Otéchestvenniye zapíski*) by Nekrásov and, after his death, by Saltykóv-Shchedrín. Literature and criticism were now in the forefront of the ideological debate and a new generation of *razno-chíntsy* writers – Gleb Uspénsky, Naúmov, Zlatovrátsky etc. – took their place alongside the liberal giants, Tolstóy and Dostoyévsky. Nekrásov in poetry and Saltykóv-Shchedrín in satire contributed their finest work at this time, and Leskóv and Mélnikov-Pechérsky began to engage the attention of the reading public.

7

The bomb that mortally wounded Alexander II on 1 March 1881 set off a chain reaction that reverberated through the entire life of the nation. Though the government wavered, there was no organised body able to usurp power, and an era of reaction and reprisal began, with savage repression of the revolutionaries, pogroms and persecution of national minorities. Russia was 'frozen a little to prevent it from going rotten'.[55] But, 'the murder of individual persons was not the way to overthrow the absolute power of the Tsar or to annihilate the landowning class', the Short History states. 'In the place of the murdered Tsar appeared another, Alexander III, under whom life became even worse for the workers and peasants.' [56]

Ironically, the success of *Naródnaya Vólya* in assassinating the Tsar led to the disintegration of the movement. Some of its members, including Lénin's ill-fated elder brother, Alexander Ulyánov, sought an agreement with the social democrats, while still clinging to their faith in terrorism; others moved towards the liberals. Thus the former drew closer to a Marxist position; the latter further away. Yet a third group attempted to maintain their original stance, and a fourth section, disillusioned, forsook all political activity.

The crisis likewise affected the opponents of *Naródnaya Vólya*, the *Chërny Peredél*. Certain of them, such as Plekhánov, Akselrod and Zasúlich, all now in emigration in Geneva, parted finally with populism and formed the Liberation of Labour movement. But not all the *Chërny Peredél* became Marxists; many turned toward the liberals and a new wave of populism arose, to be the subject of Plekhánov's attack in his article 'Our Disagreements' (*Náshi raznoglásiya*). In Lénin's view the new populists were 'disgusting reactionaries';[57] to Plekhánov they were becoming more and more an expression of 'the interests of that section of the peasantry that represents the principle of individualism and *kúlak* money-grabbing';[58] to Korolénko their philosophy was 'wretched and impoverished'.[59] Thus populism, which in the seventies had contributed so much to the development of the revolutionary movement despite its utopian nature, had by the eighties – and the arrival on the scene of Lénin – become a force for reaction.

Despite the government's repressive policies, the revolutionary movement continued to grow throughout the decade. Peasant revolts numbered more than 500 between 1883 and 1890; in 1885 the first great industrial strike took place (at the Morózov factory in the Vladímir district); student resentment at the new policy toward universities expressed itself particularly forcefully on the occasion of the fifth anniversary of Dobrolyúbov's death in 1886, after the execution of Alexander Ulyánov and other members of the *Naródnaya Vólya* terrorist fraction in 1887, and at the memorial ceremonies for Chernyshévsky in 1889. But the decisive factor was the transfer of allegiance by a significant part of the intelligentsia from populism to scientific socialism – to Marxism.

To Lénin, the 1880s were the crucial years that transformed the revolutionary movement from a loose alliance of intellectuals into the embryo of a scientific, solidly-based mass movement. 'It was precisely in this period that the old Russian populism ceased to be a visionary view of the future and conducted an examination of the economic realities of Russia which was to enrich Russian social thought. It was precisely in this period that Russian revolutionary thought became most intensive and created the basis of the social democratic outlook. Yes, we revolutionaries are far from denying the revolutionary role of reactionary periods.'[60]

The Liberation of Labour group had come into being formally on 25 September 1883, largely on the initiative of Plekhánov. Once an ideologist of populism, he had studied the achievements of Western socialists during his emigration and now, in a series of publications beginning in the 'Library of Contemporary Socialism', he attacked the renascent populism and began to outline a programme of action for the social democrats which won the acclaim of Engels. 'I am proud', Engels wrote to Zasúlich in 1885, 'that among Russian youth there is a party that has sincerely and unequivocally accepted Marx's great economic and historical theories and has broken decisively with all the anarchist and somewhat slavophil traditions of its predecessors.'[61] The group also began translating Marx and Engels into Russian, an essential step in making them accessible to the masses and a precedent for later practice. Plekhánov's programme, in fact, was to form the basis of Lénin's own programme some fifteen years later, and in these early days Lénin was effusive in his praise of

Plekhánov as the foremost Marxist philosopher of his time. But he stated, perhaps ungraciously, that the group was rather better at raising problems than it was at solving them !

8

In the period of repression that followed the assassination of the Tsar, both sections of the revolutionary movement suffered, and each was subject to attacks from resurgent slavophilism, with Aksákov as its main spokesman. The publicistic activity of both revolutionaries and liberals decreased, and reactionary journals now held the field: *Moskóvskiye védomosti* (*Moscow Chronicle*) under its editor Katkóv; *Grazhdanín* (*The Citizen*) edited now not by Dostoyévsky but by Prince Meshchérsky; *Nóvoye vrémya* (*The New Times*) under Suvórin, which catered for a wider public and which Lénin bitterly referred to as *Chegó izvólite?* (What can I do for you?) because of its servile attitudes; and especially *Nedélya* (*The Week*), edited by Gaidebúrov. The mood of the intelligentsia was confused, and the exhilaration of the preceding decade gave way to political indifference, pessimism and apathy which Gleb Uspénsky called 'spiritual paralysis'. In both ideology and the arts there was a turning away from social themes toward those of the individual.

Nedélya fostered the theory of 'little things', according to which the disorientated intellectual sought consolation in attending to details and contributing, in his small way, to alleviating the ills of society, though taking no part in any large-scale, organised movement. Tolstóy, too, repudiated his earlier philosophy and propounded his theory of non-violent resistance to evil which immediately struck a chord in the disillusioned intelligentsia. In the arts the swing away from social command brought a resurgence of interest in pure art, and the popularity of the mood of pessimism expressed in the poetry of Nádson and the stories of Gárshin.

The liberals were clearly on the defensive, trying simply to retain the gains made in the sixties, though these had never been very great. Apart from *Véstnik Evrópy* (*European Journal*), one of their foremost organs was *Rússkaya mysl'* (*Russian Thought*), which published, amongst others, Uspénsky and a new major figure, Korolénko. *Rússkiye védomosti* also published them, together with Chernyshévsky – returned from exile – and Lavróv, writing secretly from emigration. The eighties also saw the continuation of the work of Saltykóv-Shchedrín, as well as of Uspénsky, and the publication of several of Tolstóy's most powerful stories, including *The Death of Iván Ilyích* and *The Kreutzer Sonata*. A second important new writer to appear, with Korolénko, in this inauspicious decade was Antón Chékhov.

Such was the scene at the end of the second period in the history of the Russian revolutionary movement as Lénin defined it. The many contradictions inherent in the society of the eighties were to grow sharper in the next decade and to give rise to the third, proletarian, period of the revolutionary movement and to Socialist Realism in the arts.

9

First, however, the gradually emerging social democrat programme had to be embodied in a political party – a point on which Plekhánov and Lénin were agreed – and this party must have its own organ, its own voice. In fact both came about, but in reverse order, and neither in the circumstances of Russia at the turn of the century could be legal; nor did it seem likely that they could become so in the foreseeable future.

In 1895 Lénin and Mártov formed the St Petersburg Union for the Struggle for the Liberation of the Working Class (*Soyúz bor'bý za osvobozhdéniya rabóchego klássa*) and mass political agitation began. Exiled to Siberia, Lénin could not attend the first congress of social democrats which tried unsuccessfully to form a political party in 1898, but in order to provide a central platform which would unite all the various factions, he founded a new journal, *Iskra* (*The Spark*), which was in fact to become the fulcrum of discord. It began in suitable polemic style, the first issues being directed against the so-called 'economists', who denied the need for a political party. These appeared in 1900 and 1901.

Thus the profusion of journals, each with its melange of socio-political and literary interests, reflected all three streams of the revolutionary movement that were now visible – the liberal-bourgeois, the bourgeois-democratic, and the proletarian-revolutionary. The 'legal Marxists' – bourgeois elements who espoused Marxism but denied the role of the proletariat – published in *Nóvoye slóvo* (*New Word*), *Zhizn'* (*Life*) and *Nachálo* (*The Beginning*), and though Lénin stressed their essentially liberal-bourgeois outlook, he was willing to form a temporary alliance with such of them as Berdyáyev and Peter Strúve [62] in the face of more severe threats from elsewhere. The chief organ of the bourgeois-democrats was *Rússkoye bogátstvo*, edited now by Mikhailóvsky, but their point of view continued to receive the support of *Nedélya* and of the liberal populist *Rússkaya mysl'*. The liberal policy of *Véstnik Evrópy* was maintained, and an interesting and significant newcomer outside the political arena was

Séverny véstnik (*Northern Journal*), the organ of a group of writers who wanted no part in the social debates – the 'decadents' Mínsky, Merezh-kóvsky, Bálmont, Sollogúb, Gíppius, Volýnsky and the rest, who constituted the first wave of the Symbolist movement.

Of the older generation of writers, Tolstóy was still writing and Chékhov was reaching his prime. A number of gifted new authors were claiming attention – Serafimóvich, Veresáyev, Kuprín, Mamin-Sibiryák – but in literature the ascendant star was that of Maksím Górky, about to have greatness thrust upon him as the first great exponent of the new realism of the third revolutionary period. In painting, the *peredvízhniki* continued with added brilliance from Súrikov, Polénov and Levitán, and in music this was the age of Chaikóvsky.

1895, which marks the beginning of the third period, saw two meetings which were of great moment in the development of the social democratic party and its relations with other sections of society. The first was a meeting of representatives of social democrat groups from Petersburg, Moscow, Kiev and Vilnius, at which Lénin took issue with other members on a number of points, including the question of proceeding from general propaganda to active agitation of the workers. The second was in Geneva, where Lénin was sent to establish contact with the Liberation of Labour group. Through this mission the gap between the revolutionaries inside and outside the Russian Empire was bridged and a single revolutionary movement came into being.

Even so, there were visible sources of future discord. Though at Geneva Lénin and Plekhánov seem to have impressed each other greatly [63] there were points of disagreement – especially concerning attitudes to the liberals – which were later to assume utmost importance. In Lénin's independent views at both meetings we may detect the beginnings of his concept of party which was set out in *What is to be Done?* in 1902 and was soon to transform the organisational structure of the revolutionary movement and precipitate, in London in 1903, the Bolshevík/Menshevík split.

A proletarian party, clearly, requires a proletariat, and during the eighties and early nineties this had in fact come into being. Though lagging behind the West in the scope of its industrialisation, Russia outstripped it in speed and concentration, and the creation of capitalist relations and an urban proletariat – the ideal seedbed for the spread of Marxism – was accomplished with astonishing rapidity. The famine of 1892–3 and the cholera epidemic of 1893 had shaken the intelligentsia out of its apathy and brought it once again into active participation in the debate, and by the mid-nineties the country was smitten by a wave of strikes. Although by 1897 only one-sixth of the population was working outside agriculture, even half a decade later as many as three and a half million of the ten million peasant households still did not even possess a horse, and these Lénin considered 'rural proletariat', having more in common with the industrial workers than with the richer peasants. It was in such circumstances around the turn of the century that Lénin's third, proletarian, period in the development of the Russian revolutionary movement began.

* * *

Of course, history and art – unlike academic or State plans – are not made in neatly delineated quinquennia, nor in decades or centuries. Lénin himself warned against too schematic a consideration of the periods he had defined: these should not be seen as laid end to end, one beginning where the other stops, but rather as overlapping layers, perhaps of varying thickness, but all making up an increasingly complicated society. Certain years may acquire significance by virtue of some formal event, but great ideas and social movements do not arise or disappear suddenly. 1861 saw the signing of the order emancipating the serfs, but the pressure that produced this measure had been mounting throughout the entire century, and though it gradually changed in quality it continued long after the measure was passed. 1881 saw the assassination of the Tsar, but the terrorist movement had been swelling for some years before the event and was to persist for some time after it. Revolutions, too, do not happen overnight, except in the crude sense of physical assumption of power. What the Bolsheviks achieved in 1917 was a *coup d'état*; the revolution had been in train for the two previous decades and is hardly completed yet. It is not always visible in terms of violence; the Civil War of the 1920s and the Purges of the thirties represented only peaks in a fluctuating but continuous process. And in the arts the meeting of the Union of Writers in 1934 denotes only the formal institutionalisation of the 'method' of Socialist Realism that had been evolving throughout the proletarian period and must, by definition, continue to evolve. The ideological battle in the arts may indeed have reached its most spectacular peak in the twenties, but it had been in train for a century before then and is still being fought. Moreover it is not a helpful over-simplification to consider the struggles always as taking place between the Party, on the one hand, and its opponents, on the other. Implicit in the situation are the 'contradictions' within the Party, so that in any controversy or battle there is always a degree to which the Party is in fact struggling with elements in its own make-up.

As we enter our discussion of the twentieth century developments in Russia, let us first pause to sum up what we have already seen, remembering that it has not been our purpose to present a potted political history or history of art, but to point to the significant moments in the relationship between the two as an aid to our understanding of the role of the artist in Soviet society. What conclusions may we draw from looking at the first two periods that will help us understand events in the third?

First, though in the Slavophil/Westerner controversy of the first half of the nineteenth century the latter may have gained the day, we would do well to be always conscious of the former. Though the precise role of slavophilism in the populist movement can hardly be defined, its influence was clearly very great and did not cease automatically with the failure of the movement. In times of crisis its continued presence becomes noticeable, and this is still true in the latter half of the twentieth century.

Second, though in the 1860s the Westerners polarised rapidly into liberal reformers and revolutionaries, each group – in its own way – was very much preoccupied with social problems. In other words, the really fundamental division came not with the question of the role of social problems in art but with that of the identification of art with a call to revolution. Both groups were tendentious, in Engels's definition; the split concerned political orientation, explicitly a twentieth century phenomenon but having its antecedents in the aesthetics of Chernyshévsky and Dobrolyúbov, since an obligation to condemn social or political evil implies the need for a communicable and viable alternative programme.

Third, the formation of political parties came late; the focal point of both literary and socio-political debates was the journal. This was especially true with regard to the social-democratic revolutionaries; the line between 'literature' and 'publicism' was never clear, and when Lénin wrote of 'literature' in his 1905 article he made no attempt to draw such a distinction. It is of interest that the literary journal still plays a greater role in Soviet art than perhaps in any other.

Fourth, as the nineteenth century writer seemed drawn by 'reality' into the social debate, so he sometimes retreated from it into his own inner world at times of disillusion or disaster. Such a process is noticeable within the lifetime of individual artists, as well as leading to periodic movements under the banner of 'transcendental art' or 'art for art's sake'. The turn of the century was one such period.

Fifth, the crucial socio-political feature of the turn of the century was the advent of Marxism in an increasingly capitalist society. This led to fission within the intelligentsia and, through mass political agitation, the involvement of the masses in the social and political struggle. In this context art was not only to renew itself from its ancient sources in the people; it was to become a weapon in the class war.

Western Marxist theory had to be interpreted for application to the specifically Russian situation. Interpretations differed, and political and artistic groupings differed accordingly. Lénin's gloss – Marxism-Leninism – becoming the ideology of a Leninist-type party, incorporated Chernyshévsky's definition of the reforming role of art and related it to a specifically political programme. Thus the social role of art, which had been broadly accepted by the bulk of the intelligentsia at least since Belínsky, became a political role – a qualitative change that was to encounter much resistance and does so even today.

In the space of rather less than two decades at the end of the nineteenth century and the beginning of the twentieth, a general and imprecise social democratic outlook had become, with Plekhánov, a programme embodied, by Lénin, in a party. And art, which since Griboyédov and Púshkin had reflected social relations (realism), and had been directed by Chernyshévsky and Dobrolyúbov to pass judgement on those relations (critical realism) was now, on behalf of the Marxist-Leninist party, to present an alternative, socialist system of relations (Socialist Realism).

The 1903 Bolshevik/Menshevik dispute had involved the journal Iskra, and in 1905 publication of political 'literature' was legalised for the first time. It was therefore essential that the relationship between the party and the 'press' should be clarified; hence Lénin's article on 'Party Organisation and Party Literature'. In the context of his periodisation theory and the progression of the relationship of 'literature' and 'politics' in the journals of the time, the extrapolation of the principle of partiinost' as the vital force in Socialist Realism does not, perhaps, seem illogical. Such is the reasoning on which the Soviet critic's argument is based, and on such a background we shall consider the role of the artist in the Soviet Union and his artistic method, Socialist Realism.

3 A Few Decrees . . .

> We are not suggesting, of course, that this transformation of literary
> work . . . can be accomplished all at once. Far be it from us to
> advocate any kind of standardised system, or a solution by means of a
> few decrees . . .
>
> Lénin: *Party Organisation and Party Literature (1905)*

WE HAVE seen in our previous chapters how Lénin related his own political viewpoint, embodied in a party bearing his own individual stamp,
to the traditions of the nineteenth century Russian social democrats, and
how the social role of art was to become, within the context of that party,
a political role. The truly 'popular' artist was to further the cause of the
masses by integrating his efforts in those of the Party as a whole, and this
relationship was expressed in the principle of *partiinost'*. Further light
may be cast on the reason why the Party found it necessary to demand
such unquestioning support if we take a more detailed look at the argument concerning culture in general during the early years of the
Soviet era. In particular, a glance at some of the extra-artistic problems
with which the Party had to cope, and the influence those problems
exerted on its attitudes and consequent actions toward the arts, may
serve to provide a more balanced picture than we might otherwise perceive. As a basis for our discussion we may take the Party's own pronouncements, set against a background of the immediately post-revolu-
tionary decade. This was the formative period during which the Party's
policy crystallised. The Soviet critics' argument is that the policy developed logically and coherently to a point at which the formulation of the
method became a natural culmination, and we shall attempt to investigate
the evidence for such a claim.

A feature of the first quarter of the century, especially after the dis-
appointments of the 1905 revolution was, in the Marxist-Leninist view, a
crisis in bourgeois culture and the emergence in the arts of a number of
formalist movements of a reactionary nature. It is perhaps in his instinctive rather than his intellectual attitudes towards these formalist movements that the Western student evinces his first and most graphic

disagreement with his Soviet contemporaries. To the one, they are enormously exciting and stimulating; to the other – at its crudest – they are pernicious and disgusting. From the vantage point of half a century later we may now perhaps agree that as movements (in so far as they ever were coherently defined in a communicable form) they were by their own nature bound to be short-lived. On the other hand, as influences in art – both outside the Soviet Union and within it – they did not disappear without trace and are visible to the discerning eye even within the apparently totally hostile framework of Socialist Realism.

In this chapter we shall examine the evolution of the Party's policy during the early years of its power to see what evidence there is in support of the view of the genesis of Socialist Realism already presented. Let us begin with certain general statements as an introduction to our analysis of that policy.

First, the battle over formalism in the arts – no matter how loudly and colourfully it raged – was from a socio-political point of view almost incidental. To the Western student, who cannot fail to sense the exhilaration of the artistic experimentation of the times, the protagonists of the new art may seem to have occupied the centre of the historical stage. To such an observer, this was a period of unparalleled brilliance, producing ideas and personalities that have put their stamp on world art. To the workers and peasants, on the other hand, much of the debate was incomprehensible gibberish, peripheral and of no relevance to the enormous problems that confronted them, and to the ideologist it marked the final extreme of decadence, when even the elite was mystified and the gap between art and the people yawned wider than ever before. In absolute terms, it produced 'bad art'; and in terms of priorities, the whole argument was premature. The real battle was between conflicting theories of the nature of proletarian art, not between realism and formalism as such.

This battle was not joined at once, as the Central Committee's letter of 1920, concerning proletarian literature, makes clear. 'If our Party has not up to now interfered in this matter, this may be explained only by the fact that it has been engaged in military affairs at the front and has not therefore always been able to devote the necessary attention to these important questions.'[1] The importance of the issue is not denied, but its place in the scale of priorities is clearly below that of other, more pressing matters. In his introduction to *Literature and Revolution* (1923) Trótsky spelled this out more clearly, pursuing the argument eventually to the point of heresy.[2] 'Only a movement of scientific thought on a national scale and the development of a new art', he said, would signify the final success of the Revolution, but 'art needs comfort, even abundance', and the time for these was not yet ... 'The problem above all problems at the present is the economic problem.'[3] Speaking in similar vein some two years later at a debate on the early years of Soviet art,[4] the People's Commissar for Education (whose province embraced the arts[5]) supported such a point of view. 'Despite my enormous respect for art,' Lunachársky confessed, 'I can say that at this point in time a Communist must prove that he cannot engage in *anything better than art* ...' The Party was faced with 'enormous tasks of another sort', and a Communist would be directed into the arts only if he could prove his inability to make a contribution in a more productive field. And in reply to a taunt from Mayakóvsky, who had – as was his habit – turned this into an aphorism, Lunachársky brought the argument right down to the shop floor : 'If, for example, a comrade says "I am a poet" or "I am a dramatist", he may be released for a year, and if during that time he achieves great success, his release time may be prolonged. But if not, then he must be compelled to make up somehow for that year.' Art – except for the artist – was something of a peripheral matter when bellies were empty !

Second, no matter how loudly the participants sometimes shouted, the ideological argument was conducted at a primitively low level. While acknowledging that the Party's theory of literature was only then in a state of evolution, we cannot but be impressed by the apparent incomprehension of the Marxist-Leninist attitude by many of its supporters and opponents alike. Much of this chapter will be devoted to a discussion of the ideological dispute between the proletarian writers' organisations and the Party as a catalyst to the crystallisation of clear-cut principles; we shall therefore not anticipate it here. But equally good examples may be found in the other literary movements of the twenties. For Mayakóvsky and his Futurists, for example, the question of accepting or rejecting the Revolution simply did not arise;[6] they espoused what they believed it to be with 'storms of applause', but from a study of their pronouncements it quickly becomes apparent that their image of the Revolution had little in common with the real thing. Hence Lénin's energetic rebuttal of 'vulgarising sociology', a term elsewhere applied to the Proletkult but equally relevant to the Futurists. In a sense there was less danger from the frank opponent without than from the misguided sympathiser within.

The level of the argument may be illustrated by reference to the same public debate, held in 1925, at which Lunachársky analysed the progress of Soviet Literature and crossed swords with Mayakóvsky, now spokesman of *LEF* (Left Front in Art) – a development, in part, of Futurism. Though he had again been under fire not long before for discrepancies between ideology and literary practice, the Commissar delivered himself of some penetrating criticisms of other waverers. The record is not entirely coherent, and in the cut and thrust of the argument each side occasionally misrepresents the other, but the point at issue emerges quite clearly.

'Comrade Mayakóvsky says that without wasting time on reading, one can already start writing',[7] Lunachársky said: 'But I reckon this is nothing but demagogy' – a charge he was to take up again later. Then an elaborate image concerning form and content is thrown back and forth: to Mayakóvsky, the structure of the Red Army is a question of form; the bayonets and rifles are the content – and bourgeois rifles will shoot as straight as any others: the structure should therefore be changed. 'But', Lunachársky retorts, 'let Mayakóvsky take note that at several congresses we did discuss the possibility of organising the Red Army in a different way ... and we decided that if we rejected the bourgeois form and invented our own, we should be beaten.' 'For us', Lunachársky said, 'form is dictated entirely by content.' ... 'People begin to work on form as such only when they have no content.' ... 'Whenever a class has ceased to have content, the centre of the stage has been given over to formalism...' Mayakóvsky defended himself: '...this so-called formalism,' he said, 'is really a theory of production, an aid to all who already have colossal content'...; but he and LEF received a sound drubbing from an opponent clearly enjoying the vociferous support of the majority of the audience present at the debate.

We should, of course, avoid the impression that the People's Commissariat of Education was a bastion of ideological rectitude amidst a sea of waywardness and incomprehension. On the contrary, the Commissariat as first constituted was more a haven of refuge for liberal and bourgeois intellectuals whom some estimates reckon to have constituted more than half its staff. Nor was the figure of the Commissar himself above suspicion: not only was his ideological 'purity' in some doubt, but his scrupulous desire to avoid inflicting his own artistic tastes on others sometimes led him to lean over backwards and condone 'errors'. All this was acknowledged in the Central Committee's letter (1920): 'The Central Committee realises that in the field of the arts the same intellectual currents that have been exerting a disruptive influence in the Proletkults have made themselves felt up to now in the People's Commissariat of Education itself. The Central Committee will achieve the removal of these bourgeois currents from the People's Commissariat, too.'[8] Thus in some ways the history of the arts in the twenties is as much that of the Party consolidating its hold on its own apparatus as of extending its sovereignty over the artist.

A third comment, which need not be elaborated at length here, concerns the precise extent of causal relationship between the socio-political revolution and the 'revolution in the arts', since the coincidental use of the term 'revolution' probably implies a closer relationship than did in fact obtain. Certainly, as far as the Marxist-Leninist is concerned, the cultural revolution on which the Party proclaimed its embarkation in 1925 led quite naturally away from experiment and formalism in the direction of Socialist Realism – the 'art born of October'.[9] It is equally true that many revolutionaries who – as we have tried to suggest above – were quite far removed from bolshevik theory were ecstatic in greeting the collapse of the old world and hastened to proclaim a new, revolutionary, proletarian art. In a sense their efforts, too, were born of the Revolution, but not of a Marxist-Leninist sire. Thus a sort of causal relationship may be said to exist, but hardly as direct as might at first have been supposed. Nor in this context can it be true to claim that, having given rise to its own revolutionary art, the Party thereafter suppressed it. On the contrary, the Party may be seen eventually to have followed a logical line, while expressing in the early stages a commendable diffidence in matters of artistic form, together with a preoccupation with more pressing matters, as stated by Trótsky and Lunachársky in the passages already cited. It was in the process of hammering out a concrete policy that the principles subsequently elaborated as Socialist Realism were evolved.

The October Revolution, after all, came as something of a surprise, and the success of the bolshevik *coup d'état* did not, as we have suggested earlier, mean the automatic success of the Revolution. Indeed, it is difficult even over half a century later to name a date for such final 'success' – a fact that in part accounts for the waspish nature of Soviet reactions to apparent trivia even today. And when the *coup d'état* did succeed, Lénin could hardly have been said to have come to power with a roll of blueprints under his arm. It is doubtful, too, whether 'normality' is a concept that has any meaning in the Soviet Union, hurled from one crisis to another ever since it came into being. So we have to reconcile two apparently contradictory images of the Soviet communist – that of the cold, calculating planner, the 'engineer of the human soul',[10] on the one hand, and that of the basically unprepared, emotional revolutionary, reacting in near panic to circumstances beyond his control, on the other. Hence the inconsistencies and indecision sometimes apparent in the policy of the 1920s; hence, too, the importance attached to the theory of Socialist Realism as imposing a kind of order, in retrospect, on the chaotic artistic scene.

To return to the Marxist-Leninist view of literature, there is — we are told — a constant struggle within the arts in a capitalist society between the decadent and the democratic tendencies, i.e. between Lénin's 'two cultures'. At the time of the 1917 Revolutions, the decadent tendencies were very much in the ascendancy in Russia; the problem was to replace them with a new, socialist art, dedicated to the cause of the Revolution. (It is here that Maksím Górky, forming a bridge in both time and manner between the nineteenth and twentieth centuries, assumed an importance which his stature as a writer might not otherwise have justified). We may follow the evolution of the theory of socialist art from official party statements, though for a fuller understanding we must relate it to other factors also recorded for us in statements on similar themes. For whereas the theory of the role of the artist in Soviet society may indeed stem from Lénin's article of 1905, the actual practice has obviously been conditioned by reaction to other, extra-artistic circumstances, too.

In the two-pronged campaign to bring art to the masses and the masses to art, the first of these aims posed problems that were largely organisational and hence capable of more rapid solution. To this category belongs the nationalisation very soon after the Revolution of all museums, private art collections, theatres, concert halls, printing presses, libraries, etc. For a period there was no charge for entry to theatres and concerts, and tickets were distributed to factories, party cells and trade union branches. Outstanding artists were sent on tour of town and country, and mass spectacles, with folk and martial music, drew huge numbers of people into a first contact — however crude and superficial — with certain art forms.[11] The artistic achievements of past epochs were similarly brought to the view of the masses. Though passions ran high and the temptation to loot and destroy was naturally great, the new Soviet government was at great pains to preserve art treasures as part of the popular heritage. Many priceless treasures were no doubt lost, but Lénin's attitude is well illustrated by the telegram in which he replied to a query from the provinces about what should be done with confiscated works of art: 'Make a precise list of all the valuable items. Keep them in a safe place. You are responsible for their preservation. The estates become the possessions of the people. Looters must be brought to trial. Inform us of sentences.' [12]

This attitude was not simply the instinctive reaction of a cultured man – it had a deep-seated ideological motive. Lénin's belief in the organic relationship that must exist between the new, 'great, communist art' [13] that would eventually develop and the cultural heritage of pre-revolutionary epochs contrasted sharply with the nihilistic attitudes of his ideological opponents, with whom the struggle that was to take place during the ensuing decade was to be the crucible in which subsequent party policy toward the arts was compounded. For the desire to smash and destroy was also not simply instinctive fury but had an ideological basis, too. To the protagonists of such a point of view the culture of pre-revolutionary epochs must be swept away to make room for new growths,[14] whereas for Lénin 'only by a precise knowledge of the culture created by the whole development of mankind, and by a re-working of this, will it be possible to create a new, proletarian culture.' [15]

The government's concern for the safety of works of art began even before the fighting had ceased. The Moscow Soviet set up a special section under the chairmanship first of the writer Veresáyev,[16] and then of the architect Malinóvsky with, as one of its urgent tasks, that of the preservation of the Kremlin, to which many treasures had been evacuated at the outbreak of the war. This body included such universally respected figures as the painters Répin and Polénov, and it is a testimony to its success that various of the cases in which the *objets d'art* were stored remained untouched until they were officially unsealed in 1922. Similar measures were taken in Petrográd, where articles looted from the Winter Palace (now the Hermitage Museum) were sought out in a campaign directed personally by Dzerzhínsky, with the scholar, Vereshchágin, as adviser. And in both capitals and subsequently the provinces detailed inventories were made of all the property that had now passed into the hands of the State.

But theft and destruction were not the only dangers; depreciation and damage from lack of proper care were also taking their toll, and especially in the provinces a thriving black market had quickly appeared. Enormous quantities of works of art had been taken out of the country during the time of the Provisional Government, and after the Revolution many others were sold ridiculously cheaply to Western and Russian profiteers by citizens wishing to emigrate. The danger to what was now regarded as the people's rightful inheritance was countered in 1918 by two governmental measures, both over the signatures of Lénin. These were the decrees 'On the prohibition of the export of art treasures and objects of historical importance' and 'On the registration, collection and storage of art treasures and objects of historical importance in the possession of private societies and institutions'. Under the enlightened guidance of Lunachársky such measures were administered with a degree of courtesy and tact, but offenders in both cases were liable to confiscation of goods and to imprisonment.

Such measures required appropriate organisational channels, and since the inherited structure operated automatically to the advantage of the bourgeoisie, new Soviet organisations had hastily to be elaborated. The old Ministry of Education (*prosveshchéniye*) had been abolished and replaced by the People's Commissariat (*Narkomprós*) under Lunachársky and Krúpskaya, and it was to this in the first instance that the preservation of works of art was entrusted. For a short while the duties were devolved to a special commission under Malinóvsky, but by late 1918 they had again become a function of *Narkomprós* proper.

If the problems involved in bringing art to the people were to a great extent administrative and organisational, those inherent in the task of bringing the people to art were of a quite different order, requiring – it is true – certain administrative and organisational measures but demanding, above all, a considerable if unpredictable period of time. They were, in fact, largely educational, and their inclusion in the purview of the Commissariat of Education was a natural step, as asserted by the head of the section concerned with the theatre, Olga Kámeneva: 'While art is in the Commissariat of Education, the government has one aim – an educative one, to demonstrate and explain. Russia is in the stage of development when it has to be educated in art.' [17] But although the question of aesthetic training was tackled from the very outset (entry to institutions providing training in the arts was, for example, greatly facilitated for applicants from the proletariat, peasantry and Red Army), the first and major task was very much more basic; it was the elimination of illiteracy. For at the time of the Revolution, more than three-quarters of the population of the Russian Empire were totally illiterate, some forty-eight nationalities had no written tradition, and four-fifths of the children of the working class had no access to schooling.

Desperate straits required desperate measures. In November 1917 a mere matter of days after the *coup d'état*, an 'address to the people' announced the primary aim of an all-out attack on illiteracy, and although during the Civil War it proved almost impossible to proceed with this, the fighting was still raging sporadically when, in December 1919, the Council of People's Commissars (*Sovnarkóm*) proclaimed its decree 'On the liquidation of illiteracy amongst the population of the RSFSR.' [18]

and some six months later, in June 1920, an All-Russian Extraordinary Commission on the Liquidation of Illiteracy was formed to co-ordinate the campaign. At such a period every literate man was an asset, whether bourgeois or not, and his aid was to be eagerly enlisted, not spurned. Certainly the writer, who lived by the pen, acquired an enhanced status of teacher, interpreter, educator – a status that quickly became a duty in the eyes of the government and remains so even today.

In education, the reform of the school system proceeded apace, though much of its effect was doomed to be negated almost entirely by subsequent developments in the economic field. In October 1918 the Central Committee's decision 'On a unified workers' school' and the 'Declaration on a unified workers' school' published by the special State Commission on Education laid down the principles of the new, Soviet polytechnical structure. Privileged and sectarian schooling was abolished, and in contrast to bourgeois, apolitical theorists, the Party set out quite consciously 'to turn the school . . . into a weapon for the total annihilation of the division of society into classes, a weapon for the communist transformation of society'.

The three factors listed above – the preservation and display of works of art; the elimination of illiteracy and application of the new literacy to ideological tasks; and the extension and reorganisation of formal education also for ideological purposes – all required consistent and logical policies, rigorously and efficiently executed in a severely practical manner. But circumstances contrived throughout the early years of the new regime to inhibit such requirements: first, the confusion resultant on an unexpected accession to power, with the refusal of almost the entire governmental apparatus to co-operate – the period of the 'loneliness of the Bolsheviks';[19] then the Civil War and its aftermath of famine and despair; then the ideological dilemmas of the New Economic Policy . . .[20] Moreover the nature of the Bolsheviks themselves had to change if their policies were ever to be translated into practice in so inauspicious a context.

The period 1917–32 was one of momentous events; irregular, apparent advances interspersed with setbacks and daunting problems. The conventional labels, despite the danger of too tidy an ordering of confusion, are certainly convenient in highlighting major issues: 1917–18 – the establishment of Soviet power; 1919–21 – War Communism; 1921–8/9 – the New Economic Policy (NEP); 1926–9 – preparation for total industrialisation and the collectivisation of agriculture; 1929–32 – socialist advance on all fronts; (and, we might add, from 1933 – preparation for war).[21] In terms of military confrontations and social conflicts these present a confused enough picture, but in practice the complexity was further compounded by arguments within the Party itself. It is important to recall that in all spheres, and not simply in the arts, there was disagreement and discord while policies were being hammered out.

Perhaps the first major setback for the Soviet leaders was the failure of the Revolution to spread, at least on a lasting basis, to other European countries, particularly Germany. Both Lénin and Trótsky had envisaged their new, revolutionary Russia on a background of like-minded states, not as isolated in a hostile, capitalist world. But the latter was quickly to become its fate, and the Soviet regime was therefore turned in upon itself. The ensuing period of desperate rethinking and improvisation was hardly conducive to euphoric harmony as the merits of conflicting policies were vehemently argued. In such circumstances, too, there was room for the settling of private scores, adding another dimension of complication.

No one emerges unscathed from war – least of all from civil war. Although by 1921 the Interventionists and Whites had lost heart and hope and quit the battlefield, they had inflicted wounds from which the Soviet regime has not yet fully recovered. In particular the state of the economy after the war led to the adoption of a mixed system, rationalised in present-day Soviet histories [22] as Lénin's plan for the transition from capitalism to socialism, which was to last until 1928–9 and to add very severely to the Party's ideological difficulties. The isolation of the Soviet Union after the failure of the Hungarian and German revolutions led to internal dissension in the Party and the struggle between the orthodox leadership and shifting opposition groups, with which the names most commonly associated are Trótsky, Zinóvyev and Kámenev. Lénin was himself removed tragically from the scene in 1924, having been severely incapacitated for at least the previous year. All these tensions and topics are clearly reflected in the debate concerning the arts.

Yet amidst all the shifting and change of the early Soviet era the student cannot fail to be impressed by the essential continuity of the basic problem. In the twentieth century, as in the nineteenth, the central figure was still the peasant – illiterate, conservative, suspicious. In the nineteenth century he had ignored or rejected the exhortations and overtures of the *naródniki*, feeling no sense of unity or purpose on a national scale. Pressed into the First World War and caught up thereafter in the passions of the Civil War, he had returned at last to his village and been reabsorbed. Or lured or driven for a while into nascent industry, he had deserted the frozen factories and starving towns and gone home again to the land, which he now considered to have become his own. And when the land-owner was driven into emigration, the bourgeoisie destroyed and the tiny urban proletariat rendered *déclassé*, he was pampered by NEP and his eternal self-interest confirmed. Like its nineteenth century forefathers, the Communist Party – self-appointed vanguard of a proletariat still to be born – had somehow to move the peasant into its brave new world, exhorting, enticing and finally beating him into compliance, and in so doing it adopted many of his attitudes. 'Scratch a Russian,' goes the old saying, 'and you'll find a Tatar.' Scratch a Russian worker and you'll find a peasant.

Between 1920 and 1932 three major party pronouncements were made on policy toward literature: *On the Proletkults* (1920), *On the Party's policy in the field of literature* (1925), and *On the reformation of literary-artistic organisations* (1932). These, with Lénin's article *Party Organisa-tion and Party Literature* (1905) and his speech *In Memory of Hérzen* (1912) are usually quoted by Soviet literary-historians as providing the basic documentation of the evolution of *Socialist Realism* up to the first meeting of the Writers' Union in 1934, and all five documents are given in translation as appendices to this book. However, it is – as we have seen – quite misleading to consider 'artistic literature' [23] in isolation from other forms of the printed word – newspapers and journals, educa-tional publications, printed matter associated with propaganda and poli-tical agitation, etc. – all subsumed under the blanket term, 'the press' (*pechát*).[24] We shall therefore place the three statements concerned specifically with the arts in the context of a series of other statements. A fuller list is as follows:

1. On the Proletkults
     (*Letter from the Central Committee, R.C.P., 1.XII.20*)
2. Resolution on the Questions of Propaganda, the Press and Agitation
     (*XIIth Congress of R.C.P. (b), 1923*)
3. Resolution on the Press
     (*XIIIth Congress, R.C.P. (b), 1924*)
4. On the Party's Policy in the Field of Literature
     (*Resolution of the Central Committee R.C.P. (b), 18.VI.25*)
5. On the Work of the Komsomól in the Field of the Press
     (*Decision of the Central Committee R.C.P. (b), 14.VIII.25*)
6. On Measures for the Improvement of Youth and Children's
     Literature
     (*Decision of the Central Committee, A.C.P. (b), 23.VII.28*)

7. On the Statement of Part of the Siberian Writers and Literary
   Organisations against Maksím Górky
   (Decision of the Central Committee, A.C.P. (b), 25.VII.29)
8. On Publishing
   (Decision of the Central Committee, A.C.P. (b), 15.VIII.31)
9. On the *Molodáya Gvárdiya* Publishers
   (Decision of the Central Committee, A.C.P. (b), 29.VII.31)
10. On the Reformation of Literary Artistic Organisations
    (Decision of the Central Committee, A.C.P. (b), 23.IV.32)

The first of these statements concerns the relationship between the Party
and the Proletkult,[25] a topic on which we have already touched during
our discussion of the aesthetic principle of *naródnost'*. The rift between
Lénin's view and those of his opponents on this principle was extremely
deep and of the utmost importance in subsequent developments. With
Plekhánov, for whom the dispassionate study of past cultures was simply
the key to a better understanding of historical processes, Lénin now disagreed sharply, since for him the object was a severely practical one of
selecting and employing those 'progressive' elements that lent themselves
for use in building a new culture in the interests of the proletariat. Perhaps Lénin's own appraisal of Marx will serve as an appraisal of Lénin
himself: 'Everything that had been created by human society he sub-
jected to critical reworking, omitting nothing from his scrutiny. Everything that had been created by human thought he reworked, analysed
and tested out in the workers' movement, drawing conclusions that people
confined within bourgeois limitations or bound by bourgeois prejudices
had been unable to make...[26]

With the Proletkult the disagreement was even more radical though
proceeding from the same basic premises. The new proletarian culture
could not, in Lénin's opinion, appear from nowhere, invented by self-
styled specialists; it must grow organically from what had gone before. A
necessary preliminary was a general rise in the cultural level of the
masses – beginning with the Communists, but not confined to them
alone.[27] The slogan 'from each according to his abilities, to each according to his needs' implied the development of each individual to the
highest cultural level he was capable of attaining via a massive drive in
which the writer would play his part just like any other member of
society. Only from a cultured proletariat could a proletarian culture arise.
But if we anticipate a later formulation directed against one of the lead-

ing Proletkult theorists: 'To Comrade Pletnëv, proletarian culture is a sort of chemical reaction which can be produced in the Proletkult retort with the aid of a group of specially selected people. He seems to see the elements of the new proletarian culture emerging from the Proletkult studio rather as the ancient goddess appeared ready-made out of the foaming sea...' [28]

A further vital point at issue was that of the definition of 'culture' and the place within it of 'art'. Not only did the Proletkult wish to produce a 'pure' proletarian culture which could by definition embrace only a tiny part of the proletariat; it also restricted its activities to art and certain 'dubious' aspects of science. Lénin's much broader concept is made quite explicit in the opening clause of his draft resolution: 'All educational work in the Soviet Republic of workers and peasants in the field of political education in general and in the field of art in particular...' [29] Art is immediately subsumed in 'the field of political education in general' and its role is unequivocally indicated.

But the basic bone of contention was the relationship between art and politics, i.e. between the Proletkult and the Party. The leading Moscow Proletkult ideologist in 1920 was Bogdánov,[30] with whom Lénin's formerly cordial relations had greatly deteriorated, their argument having quickly transcended the bounds of aesthetics or philosophy and become political. 'Under the guise of "proletarian culture"', Lénin said. 'A. A. Bogdánov is introducing bourgeois and reactionary attitudes.' [31] Lunachársky, one of the prime organisers of the Proletkult who nevertheless opposed its attitude to the 'bourgeois' culture of the past, seems to have occupied something of an intermediate position between Bogdánov and Lénin [32] – hence the latter's clearly felt need to 'correct' Lunachársky's

---

Plate I OFFICIAL RECEPTION FOR MAKSIM GÓRKY (*see opposite page*)

KEY *Left to Right*

GÓRKY, to whom an address of welcome is being read by LUNACHARSKY; SERAFI-MOVICH with bread and salt; VERESAYEV with laurels; DEMYAN BEDNY.

Above them: TRENEV; PRISHVIN and MAYAKOVSKY. *With camera:* TRETYAKOV. *Behind him:* ASEYEV and ZOZULYA; BABEL with flowers; LEONOV. *Above them:* PILNYAK and VSEVOLOD IVANOV. *Below:* AVERBAKH with journal. *Behind him:* MIKHAIL KOLTSOV; ALEKSEY TOLSTOY; LIBEDINSKY; SEIFULLINA; FADAYEV; PODYA-CHEV; DEYEV-KHOMYAKOVSKY; GLADKOV; LYASHKO and NIKIFOROV; P. ROMANOV with flowering cherry. *Above them:* KASATKIN and SELVINSKY, *with* VERA INBER. *In the distance:* YEVDOKIMOV etc.

Plate I OFFICIAL RECEPTION FOR MAKSIM GÓRKY
A friendly cartoon by the Kukryniksy on the occasion of Górky's return from abroad in 1928.
Krásnaya Níva, No. 13, 1928.

Plate II Répin (1844–1930): The Zaporozhian Cossacks Write a Letter to the Turkish Sultan (1891)

Plate III PIMENOV (1903–): For Industrialisation! (1927)

Plate IV DEINÉKA (1899–1969): Defence of Petrograd (1928)

Plate V   JOHANSON (1893–1973): At an Old Urals Works (1937)

Plate VI YABLONSKAYA (1900–   ): Grain (1949)

Plate VII Plastóv (1893–1973): The Tractormen's Dinner (1951)

Plate VIII Gerasimov (1881–1963): For the Power of the Soviets (1957)

Plate IX Sagonek (1919–   ): Morning (1960)

attitudes on various occasions. Lunachársky relates how Lénin 'feared Bogdánovism, feared that the Proletkult might give rise to all sorts of philosophical, scientific and eventually political deviations.'[33] He had no wish to see a rival workers' organisation in competition with the Party and outside its jurisdiction. Hence his insistence that the Proletkult should be subordinated to Lunachársky's commissariat.

The text of the documents concerning the Proletkult (1920) is no doubt clear enough not to require detailed interpretation here (*Appendix III*). Perhaps, however, we would do well to note three major points arising from them, since these are of seminal importance for later developments. First, as we have just seen, the Proletkult was to be dependent on the Party; no rival proletarian organisation could be allowed to exist.[34] Second, and this marries uneasily with the first, within the Commissariat the 'reorganised workers' Proletkults' were to be guaranteed complete autonomy 'in the field of artistic creativity'. Complete autonomy without independence requires a set of finely balanced relationships not easy to achieve... And third, the work of the Proletkults was to be directed by men 'who have been closely vetted by the Party', i.e. who would ensure ideological purity, both by assisting and showing the way forward and, it must be inferred, by prohibition. It is perhaps remarkable that the word *partiinost'* does not occur in the Central Committee's letter, but the continuity of the argument from Lénin's 1905 article to the Central Committee letter of 1920 can hardly be denied. The Proletkults were in fact doomed; from the mid-twenties they passed into the purview of the trades unions, and by the early thirties they had ceased to exist formally.

Another offering 'under the guise of proletarian culture' and singled out for obloquy in the Central Committee letter because of its 'absurd, perverted tastes' was Futurism, which dated like the Proletkult from before 1917. Though of different origin from the Proletkults, the Futurists shared common attitudes with them, especially concerning 'bourgeois' culture.[35] Partly because of the enthusiasm with which most of them greeted the Revolution, Lunachársky always regarded them with some sympathy. Writing in the preface to their 1918 anthology *Rzhánoye slóvo* (*lit.: A Rye Word*) he had acknowledged that there was much in it that he could have criticised, but in particular 'in Mayakóvsky's verses there are many notes that cannot be heard with indifference by anyone young in years or at heart a revolutionary.' Nevertheless later in that same year he was to call the poet an immature youth (*nédorosl'*) who promised much in maturity, but whose maturity had been too long delayed.[36] And in the following year (1921) Mayakóvsky's poem '150 000 000' was to be labelled by Lénin as 'rubbish, stupid, absolutely silly and pretentious'; and Lunachársky, Lénin was to add, 'should be thrashed for Futurism for publishing it'.[37] The Commissariat's journal Art of the Commune (*Iskússtvo Kommúny*) became something of a platform for Futurist theoreticians, until Lunachársky found it necessary to protest.[38] Two things rather frightened him, according to his letter to the journal with reference to the Futurists; '... their destructive tendencies in relation to the past and a desire, while speaking on behalf of an individual school, to speak at the same time in the name of the authorities.' [39] This tendency by certain groups to claim a monopoly of Party approval was to be singled out for special attention in several major Party pronouncements on its policy to literature.

The 1920 Proletkult resolution and Central Committee letter were, as we have seen, largely the work of Lénin, and though he did not survive the following five crucial years in the elaboration of Soviet policy toward the arts, his influence is unmistakeable. The Party's attitude was precisely that expressed by Lénin in a letter to Clara Zetkin: 'Every artist, everyone who considers himself as such, has the right to create freely, according to his own ideals, independently of everything else. But, as you will understand, we are Communists: we cannot stand idly by and allow chaos to develop at will. We must regulate the process in a fully planned manner, and fashion its results.' [40] In so far as the Party intervened directly in matters artistic, it did so in order to support Lénin's thesis of critical assimilation of the cultural heritage and to encourage the growth of the new realism. On both these points there seems to have been full accord between Lénin and Lunachársky. In a letter to Vorónsky (of whom we shall presently hear more) in 1923 the Commissar wrote: '... I am a great protagonist of the renaissance of realism. We literally need ... realism in literature, the theatre, painting, music, poster design and graphics, the sort of realism that would proceed approximately from the *peredvízhniki*, from classical realism, but of course sharper, more demonstrative, more monumental, shading lightly into pathos on the one hand and into farce on the other.' [41]

This was the complicated and difficult period of the New Economic Policy (NEP), when the Party had to compromise many of its basic principles in order to remain in control, and in so doing gave free rein to its ideological enemies to infiltrate and openly challenge. Peasant discontent with the system of confiscation of surpluses, introduced during the Civil War in order to feed the starving towns, had been reflected at its most extreme in the Kronstadt sailors' revolt in 1921, forcing Lénin to make some highly significant changes. By substituting a system of taxation for that of confiscation he allowed the peasants to dispose of their extra produce in the open market, hence legalising private trading. Similarly in May of that year full-scale nationalisation was dropped, and in the towns as well as the villages the small trader quickly reappeared.[42] The outlook of this newly-recognised petty bourgeoisie was essentially antipathetic to all that the Party stood for; hence its preoccupation at its XIth, XIIth and XIII Congresses in 1922, '23 and '24 respectively, with combating bourgeois elements, building up its own apparatus and encouraging young proletarian writers' associations. Thus the 1922 Congress acknowledged the 'extraordinary importance of creating a literature for worker and peasant youth in order to counter the influence on them of the growing 'boulevard' literature, and to further the communist education of the masses of the youth'. And in the following year this theme was elaborated further.

The 1923 'Resolution on the Questions of Propaganda, the Press and Agitation' was a wide-ranging document comprising no fewer than 58 clauses, in 4 sections, including illuminating mentions of literature, the theatre and the cinema in contexts that illustrate both the relationship now seen to exist between the 'press' and the arts, and the very serious nature of the problems of organisation and policy that have in fact recurred throughout the whole history of the Soviet regime. It is therefore worth examination at some length.

Section I opens with a statement of organisational objectives, the unification in one system of all the activities of *komprosveshchéniye* – 'communist enlightenment', in order to transform the workers and peasants into informed, practical participants in the building of Communism, each armed with the Marxist approach. Political illiteracy must be brought to an end, and here two basic concerns are highlighted – the problem of the peasantry [43] and that of non-Russian, 'national' peoples. These are chronic problems, still acutely sensed even today in all spheres of activity, including the arts. According to the Resolution, a system of patronage (*shéfstvo*) of town over country, industrial proletariat over peasantry, was to marry the two classes in a united effort. In urban areas, extra-curricular educational activities were to be centred on the various kinds of club, and in rural areas on the reading-room, as focal points for mass propaganda and, within this framework, for *the development of creative abilities*, all under the aegis of the appropriate Party Committees. This indissoluble compound of education, political indoctrination and aesthetic training is splendidly illustrative of the philosophy that had led in the first instance to the formation of the People's Commissariat of Education, with its vast and varied brief.

In all branches of instruction, direct control by the Party was to be strengthened by centralisation of the system, the institution of agreed syllabuses, etc. This applied to the Soviet Party Schools and Communist Universities (whose aim was to train Party functionaries), voluntary Marxist circles, and courses for private study. Every specialist trained in any field must also be a skilled Marxist; enlightened, non-authoritarian teaching methods were to be elaborated and pooled via the press; special attention was to be paid to the preparation of materials for the national minorities. No less than half the Party's strength in rural areas was to be drawn into propaganda work, and special three-month courses were to be instituted to train such activists. Workers and lecturers were to be mobilised from the capital cities to service the provinces and peripheral areas (a foretaste seems detectable here of the continuing reluctance to quit Moscow or Leningrad for more distant parts of the Union.) The supreme importance of work amongst the student population was acknowledged: Communist fractions were to be formed amongst the teaching staffs; the Party's links with student organisations were to be drawn tighter; proletarian students were to be wooed and drawn into party work; the bolshevik Old Guard [44] was to train specialist cadres and form teams of lecturers; student publications were to be headed by experienced party journalists; the Socialist Academy was to extend its influence over research work; and finally: 'Since during the past two years artistic literature in Soviet Russia has grown into a great social force, spreading its influence above all on the masses of worker and peasant youth, it is essential that the Party place the question of supervision of this form of social influence on the agenda of its practical work.' (*Clause 24*)

Thus literature – and the use of the adjective 'artistic' leaves no room for doubt about what is meant – is important for the influence it may exert on the minds of the young. It must therefore come under party control. As the public becomes literate, so its reading matter must be supervised. The manner and timing of the supervision are not stated; the intention is clear.

So far the attitude to literature had seemed one of caution. Concern about the influence it might exert had resulted in a desire to control it, but as yet there had been no prescriptions concerning obligatory content or form. Section II of the 1923 Resolution deals with newspapers and journals, but once again links them with fine writing, this time in a more definite sense. The same two major problems come to the fore – the need to cater for rural readership and for the largely illiterate and backward national minorities. For both there must be more specialised publications and for the latter some expert training in producing their own. The success of the factory newspaper meant that this must also be brought under party control; publishers must co-operate, while retaining the need for commercial viability; the provincial party press must be reviewed and strengthened by contributions from the centre; Marxist classics must be published, though only in officially approved versions; and – 'Within a very short time we must complete the foundation of a publisher of special mass literature for distribution amongst the peasantry, illuminating a series of questions of interest to the rural reader *in a form accessible to him*, beginning with political education and ending with *belles lettres* and practical questions of peasant economy ...' (*Clause 40*). If one aspect of *naródnost'* – the stimulation of the creative abilities of the masses – was dealt with in Section I, then another aspect – the accessibility of art to the masses – appears in Section II with its implications of *mássovost'* (mass-ness) in the sense of simplicity of form. Not only is literature now to refuse to cater only for the elite; it must in effect cater for the semi-literate.

The deliberate enlistment of certain art forms for political purposes by stipulation of content appears in Section III of the Resolution, concerning activism or agitation, which differs from propagandising the broad aims of Communism by concentrating on more narrow and often rather transitory themes. We have already seen that insistence on such agitation was a hallmark of Lénin's concept of the Party at the turn of the century and we shall see it appear as *idéinost'* in Socialist Realism.

Certain of the traditional forms of oral agitation at mass meetings before elections, etc. were, the Resolution stated, dying out of use. In other connections, such as in explaining party policy toward land or national minorities, the need for them still persisted, and in such cases there must be improved organisation and better quality, with the training of special cadres based on rural reading rooms, etc. However, the need for detailed analyses of economic and international policies required a shift from traditional agitation to a more profound kind of propaganda: 'It is essential to put into practical form the question of the use of the theatre for the systematic mass propagandising of the ideas of Communism. For these ends it is essential ... to strengthen the work being done on the creation and selection of appropriately revolutionary repertoires, making use in the first instance of heroic episodes in the struggle of the working class.

The theatre must also be used as a vehicle of anti-religious propaganda.'
(*Clause 45*)

Coupled with the next clause, concerning the cinema, this was both an acknowledgement of and a call to the emotive and didactic power of the spectacle, which had always been recognised by the Proletkult and, was to be used with such effect by Mayakóvsky, Eisenstéin and Meyerkhóld. Like the ROSTA[45] posters of the Civil War period (which had interpreted military and political events in a graphic style that blended traditional folk figures – instantly intelligible even to the semi-literate – with an increasing obsession with the developing machine age that led along the road to constructivism and involuntary estrangement from reality), the mass spectacle was indeed an ideal vehicle for the amalgam of instruction and inspiration that was the Party's approach throughout the period until this genre, too, became mannered and estranged from the people. 'Bringing art to the masses', it involved them in a degree of audience participation hardly rivalled before or since, but the object was expressly political, the theme was dictated by a political body, and the intention to supervise and control was unequivocally stated.

Clause 46 is of particular interest as illustrating the sort of constraints under which the Party was at this time operating. During the NEP period, the Resolution stated, the cinema had grown enormously, but since the films it showed were either pre-revolutionary or made in the West, it was in fact a means of propagating bourgeois ideas.[46] The need therefore was to develop a specifically Soviet cinema by State finance and the attraction of private capital, both Russian and foreign, 'on the condition that there should be complete guarantee of ideological (*idéinyi*) direction and control by the government and the Party'. And in view of 'the enormous educative and agitational significance of the cinema' it should be infused with Communists who had worked in the industry before the Revolution, and with managers capable of putting it on a proper financial basis and ensuring that it would serve the workers entirely. The Party Congress therefore desired an immediate strengthening of *Goskinó* (State Cinema) and acknowledged the need to assist *Proletkinó* (Proletarian Cinema) in making production and revolutionary films. This last point illustrates the duality in the cinema which, like literature, reflected both the Soviet/bourgeois confrontation of the NEP period and, amongst theose who had 'accepted the Revolution', the tentative Party attitudes – based larged on essentially extra-artistic criteria – as distinct from the self-styled proletarian art of the doctrinaire Proletkult and RAPP.[47]

Section IV may at first seem of less relevance to our theme, dwelling on the role of the ex-Red Army men in carrying out propaganda in the villages, and outlining the particular need for anti-religious propaganda in national areas. Pan-Islamism, Pan-Turkism, Zionism, Roman Catholicism, Baptism, etc. were divisive forces, their clergy having more influence in the peripheral areas than had the orthodox priests in the Russian heartland. The remedy was in the schools, by applying the old maxim of 'catching them young', especially as the old activist techniques were inhibited in the national areas by the absence of a significant industrial proletariat.[48] In fact such considerations are ultimately of direct relevance, especially in view of the conclusions drawn from them, perhaps the most significant of which was that of the inescapable need for tighter centralisation and party control.

The literary scene in 1923 was one of frantic activity and complexity, being notable for the emergence of what was eventually to become RAPP and the publication of its journal, the formation of Mayakóvsky's *LEF* and the publication also of its journal, and the appearance of Trótsky's *Literature and Revolution*. The Party's own major literary effort had been directed in 1921 into the launching of the journal *Krásnaya nov'* (*Red Virgin Soil*), founded on Lénin's initiative and edited by Vorónsky, with Górky (until his emigration for health reasons) in charge of the literary section. Its policy toward the classical heritage of Russian literature was clearly that of Lénin, with full acceptance of his theory of periodisation and consequently of the significance of Górky as the first great exponent of the literature of the proletarian period. The journal's aim was to unite all those writers who had accepted the Revolution – from the 'fellow-travellers'[49] on the one hand to the peasant and proletarian writers on the other. On both these issues it was to come under vicious attack from RAPP and therefore to be provoked on occasion into vigorous self-defence.

The actual origin of RAPP dated from 7 December 1922, with the formation of the 'October' group (*Oktyábr'*) which arose because the exising organisation, VAPP, was almost defunct and its leading group, *Kúznitsa* (The Smithy) had allegedly become prey to formalist tendencies. In March 1923 a Moscow conference of proletarian writers decided to found MAPP, with the 'October' platform as its own. In close accord with the attitudes and preoccupations of the Party was the MAPP appreciation that the working class had seized political power but in general lacked even an elementary standard of culture. Equally in tune with party thinking was the realisation that a new, proletarian art would necessarily have a class nature and could not develop without the Party's active guidance. In discord, however, with the Leninist approach was MAPP's antipathetic attitude to the cultural heritage, reflecting the influence of the Proletkult. In this, from the very outset, lay one of the seeds of the ultimate destruction of RAPP by the Party. However, for the next half decade, at least, RAPP and its wrangles with other literary movements did much to clarify the Party's own policies, and the relationship between the two bodies was extremely intricate.

The first issue of the MAPP journal *On Guard* (*Na postú*), in June 1923, certainly contained much that could pass in the name of the Party. The authors attacked the various types of formalism: *imaginism* – 'the corruption of the concept of the artistic image into an autonomous, fractionalised, picturesque ornament'; *futurism* – 'the elevation of word-rhythm as such to the position of an end in itself, as a consequence of which the artist often goes off into the realm of pure word-spinning exercises, having no social significance'; *symbolism* – 'the fetish of the sound, which arose during the period of bourgeois decadence and flourished on the soil of unhealthy mysticism'. In opposition to these tendencies RAPP supported a kind of realism which, though a very narrow concept, in some ways came quite close to the Party's own ideal.

A programme of activities based on the MAPP philosophy was outlined at the Moscow conference in a lecture by Lelévich entitled 'On the Relationship with Bourgeois Literature and the Intermediate Groups', and here again we may discern the seeds of disagreement with the Party in a context of apparent accord. The socio-political background was that of NEP, with its numerous private publishing houses (more than two hundred in Moscow alone), many of which were engaged in covert anti-Soviet propaganda,[50] as well as the pornography, pessimism and mysticism that remain cardinal sins in the Soviet Union. Various of the many literary journals were opposed to the regime, and at a time when the Party was seeking peace even with the bourgeoisie some sections of the intelligentsia felt themselves in a position to exert something not far removed from blackmail.[51] In 1922 a significant group of bourgeois intellectuals (including Berdyáyev) had been driven into exile, but the Party was desperately anxious to win over the waverers, whose talent and support it badly needed. Lelévich, however, betrayed the absolute hostility of MAPP to all the fellow-travellers, including those who had by now come to accept the Revolution as an accomplished fact and were, from the Party's point of view, capable of being won over entirely. The 'vulgar sociological' criteria restated by MAPP were clearly inherited directly from the Proletkult as outlined in our earlier discussion.

Thus there were two quite basic issues on which RAPP and the Party disagreed, and in each of them the person of a major Soviet literary figure was directly involved. For if Lénin's periodisation was not accepted and proletarian literature was defined as beginning in 1917 (if not, indeed, in 1922!) then Górky fell outside it. And if the fellow-travellers must without exception be irredeemably tainted with bourgeois attitudes and therefore ultimately anti-Soviet ('Those who are not with us are against us'), then Mayakóvsky, with his Futurist past, was also beyond the pale. And what was true of Górky and Mayakóvsky must also be true of a host of lesser figures... Such conclusions were clearly not to the Party's taste.

Nor, however, were they made immediately explicit, and though RAPP was ultimately to be disbanded with all the other literary groups in 1932, it nevertheless served the Party's interests throughout the twenties by its fanatical opposition to certain other points of view. Trótsky's denial of the need for or possibility of a proletarian culture, for instance; or Vorónsky's alleged undue concentration on the fellow-travellers and consequent neglect of the rising generation of peasant and proletarian writers; the Futurist and Constructivist leanings of *LEF* and its successor, *New LEF*; *Kúznitsa*'s formalist tendencies – all these came under its lash and as a consequence some clarification of basic issues did eventually emerge. Though RAPP concentrated its sharpest blows on the establishment figure of Vorónsky and his *Krásnaya nov'* (he was indeed disgraced in 1927 but reinstated in 1930), it did become a genuinely mass movement throughout the country, even after its original journal lost touch with those masses and ceased publication, like the journal *LEF*, in 1925. And it did stand for a kind of *partíinost'*, though its definition would not have been that attempted in this book.

The Party's anxiety to mediate amongst the warring factions is illustrated by the fact that in order to prepare its next official pronouncement on literature (our third document, 'Resolution on the Press') at its XIIth Congress in 1924, it called a special meeting on questions of party policy in May of that year, inviting leading figures to attend and prepare a draft. Under the chairmanship of Yákovlev,[52] the main speakers representing the principal antagonists were Vorónsky (now editing a new journal, 'Searchlight' – *Prozhéktor*) and – for VAPP[53] and *Na postú* – Várdin, who with Lelévich and Ródov formed the triumvirate that determined RAPP policy. There were also important contributions from Lunachársky and Leopold Averbákh, a figure of some future importance. In effect, at this meeting the VAPP group attempted to have itself recognised as the official representative and spokesman of the Party, wishing the Party to accept the

VAPP line rather than seeing VAPP as conducting party policy, but this move was decisively and significantly rejected.

The importance for us of the resultant statement is the fact that the discussion of *literature* was conducted within the context of a debate concerning the *press* as a whole, of which it was now clearly felt to be a part. Though certain of the 23 clauses were concerned specifically with 'artistic' literature, it is the degree of integration rather than that of distinction that is significant, as an examination of the contents of the statement will show.

Noting with approval the progress made in the past year (*Clause 1*), the XIIth Congress thought that the link between the press and the masses must be drawn even closer, and that the press 'must concentrate its efforts on clarifying the basic problems in the life and customs of the worker and peasant millions' (*2*). Moreover 'the workers' press must satisfy the readers' needs in the general educative field' [54] (*3*) – stipulations not at all out of place in a definition of Socialist Realism in literature. In the use of language, there was a need to evolve 'a skilful combination of the maximum popular nature and expressiveness with serious and concrete relevance of content' – an equally appropriate prescription.[55] Similarly the most important function of the press was 'to educate the rising generation in the spirit of Leninism' (*4*).[56] The press must refine its means of responding to the demands of the masses; worker correspondents must be supported and protected from administrative meddling and bureaucracy, their communist education must be improved, and the constant aim must be to draw fresh cadres of workers into participation in such activities (*8*). Wall newspapers were increasing their importance and must therefore be brought under party control (*9*); the network of weekly papers must be enlarged and improved, and there must be a massive enlistment of rural correspondents and 'a skilful combination of *agit-propaganda* with the elucidation of general political and economic questions, especially concerning co-operatives and, finally, presentation intelligible to the peasantry, without false over-simplification and unnecessary vulgarisation'. Army and Navy newspapers were important and 'their content and language must be adapted to suit the youth on which the army draws'. (*10*). Publications of all sorts must be developed in the national languages, and worker and rural correspondents drawn in, with the evolution of 'the kind of newspaper suited to the level of the backward peasantry of the national republics' (*11*). Special attention must be paid to increasing the network of young worker and rural correspondents, and a major task for the *Komsomól* must be the creation of literature for the masses of the peasant youth. This must be rigorously supervised for ideological purity and concentrated on the Bolsheviks' fight against opportunism and deviation. Children's literature must also be created under similar safeguards (*12*).

An interesting new theme, in *Clause 13*, concerns the role of woman in the new society, particularly in the Muslim areas of Central Asia. Women were to be drawn into work in the press via wall newspapers, and, of course, through publication in the national languages.

Earmarked funds were to be allotted to support national, peasant and army presses, and these were to concentrate – amongst other things – on mass editions of the works of Lénin (*15*). As a matter of some urgency these were to be published in the non-Russian languages (we have already commented on the role of the stimulation of national languages in the propagation of Marxism) with special attention to editing, intelligibility, price and distribution (*16*) – all calculated to give them a maximum efficacy. The complete works were to be published in Russian, but selections only in the national languages. The numerous publishing houses were to co-ordinate their programmes more closely in order to facilitate control from the centre (*17*), and the Party was also to exercise stricter supervision of critico-bibliographic work (*18*). *Clause 19* was devoted to 'artistic' literature:

The Party's basic work in the field of artistic literature must be oriented on the creative output of workers and peasants who have become... writers in the course of the cultural rise of the broad, popular masses of the Soviet Union. The worker and rural correspondents must be regarded as reserves from which new worker and peasant writers will emerge.

The provision of support and material assistance for proletarian and peasant writers who have come into our literature – some from the lathe, some from the plough, and some from that stratum of the intelligentsia which entered the ranks of the Russian Communist Party and the *Komsomól* during the October days and the period of War Communism – must be strengthened in every way.

Special attention must be paid to the *Komsomól* writers and poets who are active in the heart of the masses of young workers.

A basic prerequisite for the growth of worker and peasant writers is more serious artistic and political study and liberation from preoccupation with narrow circles of interest, through the comprehensive assistance of the Party, especially party literary critics.

At the same time it is essential to continue the systematic support now being afforded to the most gifted of the so-called fellow-travellers, who are educating themselves in the school of comradely cooperation with the Communists. It is essential to put forward sound party criticism which, while identifying and supporting the most talented Soviet writers, will at the same time point out errors proceeding from those writers' inadequate understanding of the character of the Soviet system and guide them toward overcoming their bourgeois prejudices.

Considering that no one literary direction, school or group can or should speak in the name of the Party, the Congress underlines the necessity for regulation of the question of literary criticism and possible further party elucidation of models of artistic literature in the pages of the Soviet party press.

The Congress pays special attention to the necessity to create mass artistic literature for the workers, peasants and men of the Red Army (*19*).

The increased significance of the press demanded the enlistment of authoritative journalists; worker and peasant correspondents should be systematically trained, especially in national areas; care should also be taken in the selection of editorial boards (*20*). The increased significance of the press as a means of communication between the Party and the masses required improved mechanisms for party control (*21*), a reorganisation of the existing network of local publications (*22*), and drastic curtailment of the resources expended on departmental publications, all in the interests of providing greater support for the peasant and non-Russian press (*23*).

The importance of this rather lengthy and detailed statement is quite evident and a number of significant features are worthy of mention. First as we have said, the shape of the entire argument placing 'artistic literature' firmly within the context of the 'press' is clearly indicative of the relationship now seen to exist between them.

Secondly the preoccupation with the peasantry and non-Russian populations, the raising of their general cultural level, as well as their political literacy in particular, i.e. with the informational and instructional role of writing is continued from the previous statements we have examined. Then the extension and penetration of party control into every ramification of the press continues apace, and in the context of the VAPP/ Vorónsky dispute the Party administers something of a reprimand to each and foreshadows its later pronouncements on this theme. Heavy emphasis is put on the recruitment of worker and peasant writers via the correspondents system [57] – a tribute in part to the mass nature of some VAPP activities, though not without a lusty sideswipe at their lack of ideological and artistic sophistication and, above all, humility. The fellow-travellers are given their due in support of Vorónsky; moreover the special mention of the writers who had entered Soviet literature from a stratum of the intelligentsia, i.e. whose antecedents were not proletarian, was a direct denial of one of the major tenets of *Na postú*. The mention of literary criticism was also directed at that journal, and the reference to 'preoccupation with narrow circles of interest' is again a direct shaft at VAPP. Finally, its claim to speak in the name of the Party is expressly refuted. All these are pointers to later developments.

On 21 January 1924, Lénin had died, succumbing at last to the exhaustion that had paralysed him intermittently since late 1921, aggravated by the wounds inflicted by his would-be assassin, Dora Kaplan, in 1918. As Chairman of the Council of People's Commissars his personal authority had been immense and there was no one man of the same stature to take his place. Trótsky, who was undoubtedly nearest, had refused to become his official deputy and tended to be the focal point of opposition. To many of the Old Guard, Trótsky was a comparative newcomer to the Party, and his pro-Menshevik past was never quite forgotten. He had been on bad terms with Stálin since the Civil War, and neither was likely to be the first to hold out the olive branch nor eager, perhaps, to grasp it. Stálin had become General Secretary in 1922 on Lénin's initiative, and though that position held nothing like the power it was later to acquire, the way was clear for it to develop. Lénin's death therefore left an uneasy structure already sewn with the seeds of violent discord. There is evidence that during the last year of his life Lénin was increasingly aware of the defects in a system that was largely of his own design,[58] but despite his famous testament and dying attempt to enlist Trótsky's support to the disadvantage of Stálin, he did not succeed in preventing the further development of the policies he had himself instigated.

Certainly in the arts the continued evolution of party policy was based quite firmly on the 'Leninist' principles of *naródnost'* – critical assimilation of past culture, and *partiinost'*, each of which became relentlessly more solidly established throughout the rest of the decade. Thus the Party's next pronouncement, the 1925 decision 'On the Party's Policy in the Field of Literature' (*Appendix IV*) takes up a number of the points made in the previous year. Like the 1924 statement, it was drafted at a preliminary meeting, this time of a special commission of the Central Committee, with a very varied membership. This statement is frequently quoted by commentators on Soviet literature because of its 'liberal' tones, which are then contrasted with those of the 1932 statement.[59] It is our contention that, *taken in context*, it is in fact an integral part of a steady progression, both a summary of what has gone before and a pointer to what is to come. For in the rest of the period with which we are here concerned, as in that portion we have already examined, the severity of the problems remained unchanged and continued to dictate, as least in part, the solution offered.

The time has come – the essence of the statement runs – *when the Party has entered the field of cultural revolution.* (Clause 1). *One aspect of cultural growth has been in literature* (2). Here the contributory streams that we have seen encouraged in previous statements – worker correspondents, rural correspondents, wall-newspapers, etc. – receive honourable mention. *In the context of NEP new bourgeois elements have arisen, and these are reflected in literature* (3). *Art cannot be neutral, but it is subtle and complex* (4). *The proletariat is now in control, but its role is no longer destructive but one of 'peaceful organisational work'; it wishes to win over the intelligentsia to its own cause* (5). *It must now move into new areas, including literature* (6). *This is boundlessly complicated, for while possessing infallible criteria* (Marxism–Leninism) *for determining socio-political content, it cannot pontificate on matters of artistic form* (7). *Its policy must be determined by such factors as*: *the relationship between proletarian writers, peasant writers, fellow-travellers and the rest; its policy toward the proletarian writers themselves; the question of criticism; questions of style and form; the working out of new art forms; organisational matters* (8).

So far we have a succinct summary of the situation, though perhaps already with certain indirect reprimands for VAPP – first, that art is too subtle to be controlled by slogans, and second, that the Party wishes to win over the intelligentsia, not to antagonise it. Moreover by setting out to give a detailed statement of its policy, the Party gives the lie to the *Na postú* claim that it in fact had no policy – by which was meant simply that the Party refused to accept the VAPP general line as its own. In successive clauses the Congress set about VAPP in no uncertain terms:

The right of guidance in literature was that of the working class as a whole, and so far the proletarian writers had not earned the right to hegemony over it. The Party must assist them to do so, but peasant writers must also be supported, and the problem was to steer them onto the lines of proletarian ideology without destroying their impact on the peasantry (9). Thus, the Congress seems to be saying, the workers must give the lead to the peasants in this field, too, but so far (despite *Na postú*!) they have not proved their ability to do so... It is important here to distinguish between proletarian writers, on the one hand, and the Proletarian Writers' associations, on the other, since not all the former belonged to the latter. Obviously the Party was interested primarily in assisting writers from the masses of the industrial proletariat and peasantry; what it disputed was the right of the Proletarian Writers' associations to speak for them. To VAPP, however, the Party's refusal to recognise them in this capacity meant simply undue preference for the writers of bourgeois origin, and this was the charge they levelled at Vorónsky.

In its attitude to the fellow-travellers, the Congress bore in mind: (a) the variations among them; (b) the importance of many of them as qualified specialists in literary techniques; (c) their instability. The problem was to win them over, isolating the anti-Soviet elements – now of insignificant proportions (10). This was anathema to the adherents of *Na postú*, who denied that bourgeois writers, however skilled, could contribute anything of value to proletarian literature, who saw counter-revolutionaries under every stone, and who seemed to set out to alienate the fellow-travellers who might otherwise have joined cause with the Bolsheviks.

In its relations with the proletarian writers, the Party must offer them and their organisations all possible help, but it warned against the fatal consequences of 'komchvánstvo'. *Seeing the proletarians as the future leaders, the Party was adamant that they should not neglect the cultural heritage; it therefore opposed both* 'kapitulyánstvo', *on the one hand, and* komchvánstvo, *on the other, as well as artificial 'hot-house' proletarian culture (11).* The charge of *komchvánstvo* ('communist conceit') was a very serious one frequently levelled at *Na postú* for its claim to be the repository of all wisdom concerning proletarian literature. (It was also made by Lunachársky with reference to Mayakóvsky).[60] The consequence was a compound of narrow-minded sectarianism and complacency, which critics described as fatal. Moreover in this context it involved rejection of the Leninist critical assimilation of the culture of the past. The invented term *kapitulyánstvo*[61] was here applied to Trótsky's attitude of postponing the question of the new art until the formation of a classless society in which, since there would be no classes, there would be no class art, proletarian or otherwise. (Though Vorónsky did not share this view entirely, his alleged undue attention to the fellow-travellers brought him under suspicion, and any stick was good enough for VAPP to beat him with). The reference in this clause to 'hot-house' proletarian culture is a clear echo of the argument concerning the revival of the Proletkult in 1922. In fact the personnel of VAPP coincided partly with that of the old Proletkult.

All this went to determine the role of criticism, one of the Party's most important educative media. While rigorously preserving ideological purity, critics should be tactful in pointing out errors and wooing potential supporters, avoiding pretentions, semi-literate and smug komchvánstvo (12). This is strong stuff! Taking up the point already made in the 1924 statement, the Congress now couches it in far more explicit terms. 'Pretentious, semi-literate and smug' – the adherents of the *Na postú* line are reminded that they are only self-styled experts, open to serious questioning concerning their real abilities and knowledge, as well as for their arrogance. And Vorónsky's repeated objections to the tone of the *Na postú* criticism finds official support.

Having analysed the socio-class content of the various literary movements, the Party cannot give its support to any one of them 'in the field of literary form'. *The Party believes that a style appropriate to the epoch will emerge, but as yet this problem has not been solved, and attempts to bind the Party to any one faction will be rebuffed* (13). Again the target is VAPP, whose claim to have evolved new proletarian art forms is denied, together with their desire to be recognised as party spokesmen in the arts. But the shaft also found its mark in the more experimental, formalist movements whose emphasis on the 'revolution in art' implied a negation of the Leninist assessment of the cultural heritage and had led to the evolution of new forms of elitist art, equally inaccessible, with the old, to the masses. There is, perhaps, something a trifle disingenuous in the Party's repeated disclaimer of any desire to make stipulations concerning form; we shall return to this point in a moment.

Therefore the Party must declare in favour of free competition in this field. No group or organisation may be granted a legal monopoly in literature or publishing via a party decree (14). This is really spelling the message out. The RAPP technique of deliberately misunderstanding or misinterpreting party intentions is the target here, though the shaft was, as usual, evaded.

Attempts at self-appointed and incompetent administrative interference in literature must be eradicated (15). The *Na postú* ruling that forbade members of VAPP to publish elsewhere, and similar 'restrictive practices' are outlawed.

The final clause (16) is an interesting pointer toward the future and highlights a problem very real in the context of the Union of Writers today: *there must be a clear line of demarcation between the functions of the critic and those of the writer*. We may interpret this as a reference to a problem that was of growing concern even within VAPP to a body of members, especially those grouped around Fúrmanov. Although it might seem obvious that wrangles over the nature of proletarian literature and the institutionalisation of the various schools of thought would take second place to the actual function of literary creation, this was not the case in practice. Writers became more and more involved in a multitude of committees, so that they tended either to stop writing or, if they wished to concentrate on their work, to opt out of the discussions. Both courses were equally disadvantageous to the cause, but the Party, while encouraging writers to write, was incidentally stimulating the emergence of the sort of literary bureaucracy of which, in theory, it disapproved. While *concentrating on 'literary production in the real sense of the word'* (?), *the writers must make use of 'the gigantic material of contemporary times'*. The insistence on preoccupation with problems of the day (though not to the exclusion of, for instance, the historical novel, which has an obvious relevance to the modern scene) which is a hall-mark of Socialist Realism, appears here almost incidentally, as does the need for *'increased attention to the development of national literatures'*, which we have seen to be an essential ingredient in any pronouncement. Both are now so obvious that they need not be stressed.

In the final two brief paragraphs we return to the vital topic of intelligibility to the masses. In its references to art forms, the Party was at pains to stress its appreciation of the 'specifics' of the literary process, and of its own incompetence to pontificate on matters of form and style. But the implications of its insistence on intelligibility to a semi-literate readership ('bringing art to the people') are clearly very great indeed. *Only when Soviet literature has worked out a form intelligible to the millions*, the statement concludes in italics, *will it have fulfilled its historic cultural mission*. In other words, the Party does not insist on any specific forms, nor veto any others, so long as art is intelligible to a mass audience, not to the 'upper ten thousand'. But by virtue of this stipulation alone, any kind of experimental art, any attempt to carry out the 'revolution in art' that so fired the imagination of the 'formalists', was ruled out of court.

The immediate effect of the 1925 statement, foreshadowed though it had been by the previous statement on the press, was to give much relief to the movements other than VAPP, and a severe jolt to that organisation itself. Two major results are worthy of our attention here. First, on 14 June 1925, the formation of a Federation of Soviet Writers was announced,[62] with the following aims: (1) cooperation in the class struggle on the literary front; (2) the eradication of *kapitulyánstvo* and *komchvánstvo*; (3) the exchange of theoretical and creative experience; (4) cooperative publishing; (5) organisational measures to improve the artistic qualifications of youth. In fact this was never to be a very effective body, due largely to the obstructive attitude of VAPP, but it was nevertheless a significant step toward the formation of the Writers' Union which, like the Federation, embraces party members and non-members alike. Second, within the ranks of VAPP the growing discord centred around the figure of Fúrmanov (who died in 1926) came to a head, resulting eventually in the removal of the triumvirate (Várdin, Lelévich and Ródov) from their all-powerful position. However, this too was only a partly successful measure, since Averbákh, who inherited their mantle, was in many ways a continuer of their policies. Even so the original *Oktyábr'* platform was re-examined and revised, though there remained a considerable gap between theory and practice, in that old habits died hard. In general it may be said that whereas Várdin, Lelévich and Ródov considered the 1925 statement spelled the end for VAPP and therefore opposed it, Averbákh (supported by Fadéyev) chose to regard it as approving much of the VAPP general line and tried to adapt it to suit the rest. Under his aegis VAPP began to be more concerned with literary theory and less with organisational and political polemics, attempting to apply Marxist theory to literature to produce a 'dialectical materialist artistic method'. Their mentor, however, was not Lénin but Plekhánov, and in this they again began to deviate from the party line.

In the four party statements examined so far we have already seen the seminal stages of the principles embodied in the theory of Socialist Realism. Indeed, all the fundamental roots are already there, and their growth or mutation in response to developing or changing circumstances need occasion very little surprise. These processes are clearly visible in subsequent party pronouncements.

Some two months after the approval by the Party Congress of its statement on policy toward literature, the Central Committee published its resolution 'On the Work of the *Komsomól* [63] in the Field of the Press' (14 August 1925) in which it elaborated the points made in Clause 12, etc. of its 1924 statement. This spells out, among other things, the overall aims of the *Komsomól* press and the topics on which it should concentrate, and makes interesting reading in the light of the *idéinost'* – preoccupation with 'concrete' current problems – required of socialist-realist literature.

A mass newspaper, *Komsomól'skaya Právda*, was to be started, closely linked with the *Komsomól* Central Committee and with *Právda* (*3*). This was to be accompanied by a theoretical journal concerned with problems of the youth organisations, Party policies, the Comintern, etc. where appropriate, in national languages (*4*). The peasant element must be strengthened and the press must work toward worker–peasant unity under the guidance of the proletariat (*5*). The enormous size of the young correspondents' movement in town and country necessitated increased party interest in them (*6*). The growth of wall newspapers equally required attention; rural versions must concentrate on explaining party agricultural policy, etc. (*7*). There was an urgent need for books for youth – explanations of the principles of Leninism, the history of the revolutionary movement, the Civil War, international relations; '*Artistic literature has great significance for worker and peasant youth, and in accordance with the Central Committee's directive on literature, attention must be paid to its creation*'.* There was also need for books on technical subjects, professional training and *Komsomól* activities (*8*). The provision of books for the peasant youth was especially important (*9*). Series of popular brochures must be compiled for *Komsomól* use in rural areas on such topics as: Soviet decrees; agriculture; financial questions; the structure of the Soviet system; the functioning of cooperatives, collective economy, etc.; the campaign to liquidate illiteracy; the *Komsomól* system; worker and peasant unity; the October Revolution, etc. (*10*). The *Molodáya Gvárdiya* (Young Guard) publishers were to be made correspondingly stronger (*11*). Mass series issued via periodicals must encourage systematic reading (*13*). *Komsomól* journals should specialise on certain types of readership; *Sména* (Shift) – on worker youth; *Peasant Youth Journal* – rural youth, both party members and non-members; '*The journals must become focal points for groups of young poets and writers, young correspondents, etc.*' * (*14*). Increased attention must be paid to catering for the needs of non-Russian minorities (*15*).

The enormous importance of the role assigned to youth, the attention devoted to it in the early days of the Soviet regime,[64] and the prominent part its representatives were exhorted to play in subsequent political, social and artistic developments are all to be seen in this statement. The publications mentioned have long since become household names in the Soviet Union; a large number of outstanding modern writers began their literary careers through *Komsomól* journals, and from the point of view of theme (industrialisation, collectivisation, etc.), genre (the novella and the novel), and style (a tendency to black-and-white characterisation, simplicity of language and imagery, pointing of the moral at the end of a story, etc.), the determining factor of the informational and indoctrinating role assigned to the sequence – newspaper/journal/popular brochure/ mass literary series – is readily visible.

Further evidence of the importance attached to the ideological training of the young via written works is provided by the Central Committee decision 'On Measures for the Improvement of Youth and Children's Literature' of 23 July 1928:

The *Komsomól* and children's press had increased and improved (*Clause 1*). But it had severe faults: (*a*) it was ideologically weak in criticising harmful new tendencies, prone to sensationalism, and neglected newcomers from school to work; (*b*) it was extremely inadequate in rural areas; (*c*) artistic literature for youth was still expensive and of poor quality (it often contained elements of unhealthy adventure-seeking and an inability to illuminate social themes); (*d*) in children's literature the least satisfactory features were – inadequate discussion or even avoidance of social themes, high price, orientation on the better-off social strata, dryness and absence of attractive, lively plots; crude tendentiousness. (*2*). The basic tasks of the press for youth and children must be the communist education of worker and peasant youth, inspiring them with the militant traditions of bolshevism, attracting them into active participation in the building of socialism via the young correspondents, etc., instilling proletarian class intolerance of negative social phenomena, with a general raising of the cultural level, etc. (*3*); It was essential: (*a*) to guarantee artistic literature responding to the social and everyday interests of youth, plus popular scientific and technical books; (*b*) to pay special attention to popular series for the peasant masses (*c*) to improve the relationship of *Komsomól'skaya Právda* with the Party, together with its elucidation of the Party's work in rural and national areas, concentrating on positive aspects of the building of socialism; (*d*) to improve the system of financing; (*e*) to increase the volume of publications in national languages; (*f*) to extend and improve the publication of children's literature 'with special attention to the creation of books promoting the rearing of children in the spirit of collectivism and internationalism'.

The line between 'artistic literature' and journalism is now totally blurred; there is a demand for ideological purity, preoccupation with contemporary themes, the usual attention to rural and non-Russian populations, and the need for a degree of artistry in presentation that will avoid crude schematisation (an accusation often made of RAPP writers) to produce a more effective medium for conveying its socio-political, ideological content. There is a quite unravellable melange of interests:

organisational, economic, ideological and aesthetic – all of which is typical also of the present day.

The intervening years between these last two policy statements had seen a number of important developments. In particular the struggle between Stálin and Trótsky had reached a dénouement. United in opposition to Stálin and Bukhárin, the triumvirate of Trótsky, Zinóvyev and Kámenev had been ever-mindful of Lénin's prohibition of factions [65] and, in their anxiety not to commit the ultimate crime of splitting the Party, they had fought with one hand tied and had consequently been divided and destroyed. Though their differences had concerned wages and the pace and timing of industrialisation and the collectivisation of agriculture, with also the question of bureaucracy and democratic procedure within the Party, the argument became polarised about the issue of 'Socialism in One Country' – the Stalinist insistence that the Soviet Union must become totally independent in a capitalist world. Giving up the dream of world revolution meant, in Trótsky's eyes, not only the failure of the Revolution but betrayal of the Comintern and resorting to improbable alliances with bourgeois forces against the interests of brother Marxists.[66] So anxious was Stálin to placate the capitalists and avoid provoking war that he was prepared to risk seeing the Chinese Communists destroyed by an increasingly reactionary Chiang Kai-shek in a Kuomintang that had swerved sharply to the right; and in the Anglo-Soviet Council the Bolsheviks were hobnobbing with reformist trade unionists who were playing the capitalist game, even to the extent of cooperating in breaking the 1926 General Strike. To Stálin, however, all this was simply symbolic of Trótsky's abstract and unreal appreciation of precise conditions; what the masses wanted was not permanent revolution and a United States of Europe, but peace and prosperity at home. Although in fact Trótsky's forebodings about events in China proved justified (tens of thousands of Chinest Communists were slaughtered in Shanghai in April 1927); the Anglo-Soviet Council disintegrated (indeed, in May the British police raided the Soviet trade mission in London and the Conservative Government broke off diplomatic relations with the Soviet Union); and elements of the opposition's industrial and agricultural policies were in fact adopted or invalidated by Bukhárin [67] and Stálin (in October, for example, they proclaimed a 7-hour working day and a 5-day week, neither of which was practicable), the latter were able to manoeuvre their opponents into untenable positions and, in January 1928, to exile Trótsky to Almá-Atá, from whence he later left the country altogether. We cannot dwell on these issues here, but it is important always to bear in mind that such were the portentous events of which the Party's debates on the role of the arts formed part of the background in the period under discussion. Stálin's victory over Trótsky was not simply that of one aspiring leader over another – as subsequent developments might suggest. Above all it was a victory for Lénin's concept of the Party and the principle of *partíinost'* – a victory ironic in that it was inflicted by one whom Lénin had with his dying breath disowned over one to whom he had *in extremis* turned for support.

In the literary debates throughout this period the same processes were at work. The 1926 VAPP plenum had decided it was essential 'to open a discussion on questions of the artistic platform',[68] which showed it was taking some heed of the Party's exhortation to devote itself more to literary theory and less to organisational and political polemics, but the discussion it proposed was to be conducted 'on the basis of the heritage of Marx and Plekhánov, the basis of dialectical materialism'. This was the beginning of the evolution of the 'dialectical materialist artistic method' to which, according to some critics,[69] the theory of Socialist Realism was needed as a deliberate counter. In 1927 according to the report in the new journal, the MAPP conference showed both the strength and the weakness of the new direction in which that organisation had embarked after the shocks of 1925: 'The conference's main attention was occupied by the question of the creative paths of proletarian literature. There is no doubt that proletarian literature will develop along the line of artistic realism ... We mean a new, proletarian artistic realism, which has assimilated the achievements of world literature and is developing along special paths ... The path of the psychological revelation of the living man – such is the path of proletarian realism ...'[70]

The adherence to realism was not new, but the 'assimilation of the achievements of world literature' and preoccupation with psychological revelation of character à la Tolstóy[71] were steps that took VAPP, from the point of view of the Party, in the right direction.

At the first congress of proletarian writers, in 1928, it was decided to form an All-Union League of Associations of Proletarian Writers, VOAPP, but this remained largely a cipher, the real power being concentrated in the equally newly formed RAPP, with Averbákh at the helm. The conference was notable for fierce debates on the 'artistic platform', which now had a number of planks, some of which were distinctly unstable from the ideological aspect. The role of revolutionary romanticism (whose antecedents in the nineteenth century democrats we have already seen)[72] was, for example, denied in the RAPP concept of proletarian

realism. The debates did not, however, result in the formulation of a
comprehensive programme, and the desperate passion with which RAPP
theoreticians espoused certain principles as 'critical' or 'decisive' suggests
a fundamental lack of confidence and certainty.

Indeed, as the 1925 statement had reminded them, the RAPP leaders
were in fact only self-appointed experts, and they were now facing the
challenge of highly trained products of the party schools and other establishments set up after the Revolution.[73] If their skill as literary craftsmen
had always been reckoned inferior to that of the fellow-travellers (the
perhaps not flattering cause of another dimension in their antipathy), their
ideological weaknesses were now being equally exposed. Moreover the
other literary movements were gaining maturity and becoming more
ideologically acceptable without suffering from RAPP's arrogant dog-
matism.

Within the Federation of Soviet Writers – which was not able to hold
its inaugural meeting until 1927 because of the tactics employed by RAPP,
the organisation continued its polemics. Although in theory all member
associations had joined on equal terms, RAPP again claimed a right to
the leading role in the name of the proletariat. Its vicious attacks on
Vorónsky were crowned with apparent success when the latter fell from
grace in 1927 in association with the downfall of Trótsky. But it also
aimed its sights at rather less vulnerable figures, including that of Maksím
Górky.

The RAPP attitude in fact occasioned the publication of a special
Central Committee statement in 1929, directed at the perhaps surprising
target of the Siberian writers' associations. Their attack on Górky,[74]
whom they considered a fellow-traveller who had 'got off' at the bourgeois revolution of February, 1917 had begun in 1928 in a speech by
Yermílov [75] accusing him of individualism, an equivocal attitude to the
intelligentsia, antipathy to the peasantry, and *humanism* – by which was
meant an anti-collective position. Górky's return to the USSR in that
year was the occasion of rapture and eulogy (*see* Plate I) but *Na
literatúrnom postú* alleged that he was unreliable, and Averbákh led an
onslaught on him for his defence, in *Právda*, of a minor poet, Molchánov
(who was also to be lampooned by Mayakóvsky in *Klop – The Bedbug*).
In fact Górky's point had simply been that such inexpert writers should
be treated tactfully and aided, rather than being ruthlessly destroyed
by RAPP ('valued and taught, not yelled and barked at'),[76] but this
marked the start of a crusade in which Molchánov was a pretext rather
than a cause. Górky was now accused of condescension and conceit, and

his total loyalty to the proletariat was questioned. *Právda* took Górky's part, but Averbákh's attacks in *Na literatúrnom postú* were echoed in the journal *Nastoyáshcheye* (*The Present*), published by the Siberian writers' organisation, which had been founded by none other than Ródov (formerly of the VAPP triumvirate) and whose editor, Kurs, was an admirer and emulator of Averbákh. In tirades of mounting fury Górky was called a class enemy and said to be protector of anti-Soviet elements. At this point the Party stepped in with a resolution 'On the Statement of Part of the Siberian Writers and Literary Organisations against Maksím Górky' (25 July 1929):

Leaving a detailed discussion of the basic arguments to be dealt with in another statement, the Central Committee considered 'grossly mistaken and bordering on hooliganism' the description of Górky's position as that of 'a crafty, disguised enemy' (Siberian Proletkult, *Nastoyáshcheye*, Nos. 8 and 9, 1929); the accusation that he was becoming ever more frequently 'a cover for the whole reactionary section of Soviet literature (*Nastoyáshcheye*, 5, 6 and 7); and that he was a defender of 'Soviet *pilnyakóvshchina*[77] in all its manifestations, i.e. not only on the literary front' (*Soviet Siberia*, No. 218). Such attitudes betrayed the distorted literary-political line of various Siberian associations (the *Nastoyáshcheye* group, the Proletkult, the Siberian APP) in their attitude to Górky. The Central Committee therefore resolved:

(1) To administer a firm reprimand to the Communist faction of the Siberian Proletkult.

(2) To demand an explanation from the editorial board of *Nastoyáshcheye*.

(3) To remove Kurs from his duties as *de facto* editor of *Nastoyáshcheye* and *Soviet Siberia*.

Moreover the Siberian Party Committee was instructed to strengthen the leadership of the Siberian literary organisations to ensure the conduct of the struggle against 'left-wing' deviations, as well as against bourgeois influences.

This whole incident is interesting for a number of reasons: the nature and tone of the accusations levelled at Górky are illustrative of the tenor of literary-political arguments in the late twenties (and in the two successive decades, at least); the common attitudes of Proletkult and RAPP are again highlighted; and finally, the very fact that the statement was thought necessary is evidence both of the Party's relationship with Górky and of the rift between the Party and RAPP on the subject of Górky and proletarian literature.

It is quite certain that Górky's role in the formulation of the method of Socialist Realism has been overstated by its protagonists and critics alike, and the image of him and Stálin together plotting a means of dragooning the wretched writers is hardly a credible one. But it is obvious that without the inclusion of Górky, Lénin's whole periodisation theory is much impoverished. It *needed* the figure of Górky as a bridge between the *raznochíntsy* and the Soviet writers; hence the Party's wooing of him and its vehemence in taking the unusual step of rebuking the Siberian writers in so formal a manner. He was perhaps used as a stick with which to beat the 'left', but to represent him as a senile 'veteran' – at the age only of 64 in 1932! – is not an argument likely to find sympathy with many writers.

Some indication of Górky's activities after his return to the USSR in 1928 is given by two further Central Committee decisions, each giving blessing to a large-scale publishing project designed by him. Thus on 30 July 1931, the Party approved his project for a *History of the Civil War (1917–1921)*, in ten to fifteen volumes in the form of scientific-historical articles and literary-artistic works, and on the 10 October of the same year it granted him permission to proceed with 'the publication of a series of anthologies, *A History of Factories*,[78] designed to portray the development of old factories and the arising of new ones, their role in the economy, the position of the workers before the Revolution, the forms and methods of exploitation in the old factories, the workers' struggle with the entrepreneurs, their living conditions, the appearance of revolutionary movements and the role of each factory in the revolutionary movement, the changed situation after the Revolution, the changed type of worker, the shock-worker system, socialist competition and the rise in productivity in recent years'. The workers themselves, managers and engineering and technical staff were to be involved in the compilation. All this semi-factual, semi-artistic documentation of the Marxist-Leninist view of recent history is very much in harmony with the tenets of Socialist Realism.

More vulnerable because of the sensitivity and lack of confidence that lay behind his bluster was Vladímir Mayakóvsky, who applied for admission to RAPP in 1928 in order to show his solidarity with the other proletarian writers, with whom he had always loudly claimed a kinship that was, in fact, demonstrably non-existent. This was a big fish for RAPP to net and they played it for all they were worth, subjecting Mayakóvsky to public indignity in demanding disavowal of his former allegiances at the meeting at which he was admitted. Forsaking his puzzled and indignant sympathisers, he isolated himself voluntarily in a sea of hostility, and there was certainly no question of rescue by the Party. Precisely what precipitated his suicide in 1930 will probably never be known; his private life was astonishingly incompetent, and hitting out at the entire establishment in *Klop* and *Bánya* (*The Baths*) must have left him with few friends he so urgently needed, but amongst the small fry of RAPP he inspired an awful fear, and it is a measure of their alienation that they did not recognise or would not acknowledge his genius.

There is much that is ironic in the fate of Mayakóvsky – not least the fact that it was Stálin who rescued him, posthumously, from ignominy, though it would have been Stálin who, had Mayakóvsky survived his own hand, would certainly have hounded him to the grave. It is ironic, too, that it is his most vociferous adulators who have done most violence to his memory. But perhaps the supreme irony of the whole period is the fact that whereas RAPP, by its high-handed activities and manner, made its own liquidation inevitable, many of its basic attitudes to the role of literature and the writer were to survive its own demise.

This, however, was not yet to be foreseen. In its ideological battles at the end of the decade RAPP was crowned with evident success,[79] though in fact it had the support of party theoreticians in some of them and could therefore hardly be justified in claiming victory as its own. But against its internal opposition – the Literary Front (*Litfrónt*) RAPP gained only a pyrrhic victory, for although *Litfrónt* dissolved itself voluntarily in November 1930, at least some of the leading members of RAPP began to sense the inevitable need for reorganisation within their own ranks. In a curious way, RAPP was now fighting the Party's battles for it, and in proportion as it was successful, it rendered itself redundant. Certainly by the time the Party made its next relevant pronouncement in 1931 the situation in all branches of the life of the country was undergoing a radical change, while RAPP was either being left behind or was making violent but pathetic gestures of modernity. Hence its order to its members to show proof 'within two weeks' that each was engaged in portraying 'the heroes of the five-year plan' – an incredibly naïve and simplistic response to the Party's call for universal participation in the 'great leap forward'.

The period 1929–32 was a vital one, in which the first great Five-Year Plan had been adopted and was completed before time at the cost of untold heroism, laying the basis for the full-scale 'building of socialism' that was to come. In agriculture, the programme of forced collectivisation destroyed the class of *kulaks* – peasants who employed others – which had prospered under NEP, though only after struggles reminiscent of the Civil War. And in matters of art, it was no longer Lunachársky who spoke for the Party but Andréi Zhdánov.

In the meantime the Party's policy toward the 'press' had begun to emerge even more clearly and to take on a more imperative tone. Much of the Central Committee decision 'On Publishing (15 August 1931)' concerns details of organisation that need not engage us here, but the relentless progression toward Socialist Realism as we now know it, within the new circumstances following the end of NEP, is certainly relevant.

The preamble to the statement outlines 'the gigantic rise [80] in the political and cultural level of the workers and collectivised peasantry founded on the strengthening and broadening of the material bases of socialism' and the consequent increased demand for reading matter. It then states quite baldly that *'the development of the cultural revolution increases the educative role of artistic literature'*. A general list of achievements is followed by an even longer catalogue of defects, publishers are urged to face the new problems by specialising, and then a general statement relating to 'the book' (*kníga*) provides both a summary and a prognosis:

> The character and content of the book must correspond entirely to the tasks of socialist reconstruction. The book must be militant and concerned with current policies. It must arm the broadest masses of the builders of socialism with Marxist-Leninist theory and a knowledge of production techniques. The book must be the most powerful medium for the education, mobilisation and organization of the masses around the tasks of economic and cultural construction. The quality of the book must meet the ever-growing cultural needs of the masses.
>
> In type, content and language the book must meet its specific objective and the level and interests of the readership for which it is intended.

Under the heading *The Organisation of Publishing*, a scheme for specialisation is outlined (an interesting point is that provision for the basic needs of national minorities is now thought generally adequate), and under *On the Tasks of Publishing* the specialised publishers' programmes are sketched in. For one of them, OGIZ,[81] there is a return to the opening theme: 'Artistic literature, which plays an enormous educative role, must give a deeper and fuller depiction of the heroism of socialist construction and the class struggle, the transformation of social relations and the growth of the new men – the heroes of socialist construction . . .'

Further: 'All publishing must be conducted in the name of all-round assistance in the building of socialism, raising theory to a higher level and combining it with practice, organising and mobilising the masses for socialist construction, the unmasking of bourgeois and petty bourgeois ideologies and the struggle against such ideologies and against deviations from the Leninist line. Publishing must also proceed from the problem of the international education of the masses.'

The third section deals with *Periodical Literature* and gives a splendidly succinct summary of the chaos that had arisen under NEP and which the Party was now setting out, by firm organisational measures, to reduce to some sort of order: 'Noting that the quality of journals published is still on a low level, journals are frequently not militant, have no firm programmes, duplicate each other, suffer from inferior authors' cadres, do not appear on time, etc. . . .' This is cited simply as an illustration of the need for drastic measures if Lénin's 1905 precepts were to be met and this type of literature was to become 'a component of organised, planned and integrated' party work.

One of the problems mentioned is that of the poor quality of authors and editors, and this topic is taken up in the fifth section *On Authors' and Publishers' Editors' Cadres*. The first comment in this section seems worth quoting in full, since it goes some way toward stating the case for a Writers' Union: 'The gigantic growth of the country, accompanied by the rapid political development of the working class and collectivised peasantry, has produced hundreds and thousands of talented writers in the fields of theory, art and technology. All this poses a severe problem for the publishers: how to assemble and organise all the newly growing forces of authors and to help them to rise to a higher level of culture, knowledge and specialisation.'

The measures proposed included selection of the best writers for preferential treatment in the sense of better conditions for work and study; the introduction of salary differentials as a means of rewarding merit and stimulating activity in certain fields; the provision of consultation for aspiring authors; improvement of editorial boards by the institution of courses of training, etc. – various of which are now within the purview of the Union of Writers.

In subsequent sections the statement reiterates previous comments on the role of the critic in ensuring ideological purity, and emphasises the unsatisfactory state of work in the field of bibliography. It then deals with problems of printing, paper supply and distribution, and ends with an oblique statement of the publishers' ultimate aims: 'The Central Committee considers that the fulfilment of the above tasks requires the strengthening of publishers by qualified and tested workers who will guarantee the success of the struggle against bourgeois and petty bourgeois ideologies, the struggle for the Party's general line.'

All this is drawing very close indeed to a draft of the principles of Socialist Realism, and this is equally true of the one remaining party statement that we shall examine before the 1932 decision to create one comprehensive union. This is the Central Committee decision 'On the *Molodáya Gvárdiya* Publishers' (29 December 1931), which relates very closely to statements we have already analysed and draws them together in one final synthesis. The penchant for superlatives noticeable in this period and the beginning of the style of invective typical of the thirties and immediately post-war periods (and, indeed of *Na postú*) are also obvious. The statement opens in quite unambiguous terms: 'At this stage of history, the struggle for the bolshevik education of young people and children in the spirit of Leninism, and for the international upbringing of the proletarian and collectivised peasant youth of the Soviet Union requires exceptional attention to the sharpest bolshevik weapon on the ideological front – literature for young people and children.'

Molodáya Gvárdiya has had certain successes, especially organisational but has many serious defects. It has published politically harmful books, departing from current ideological teaching, and others that are unhelpful; it has served the *Komsomól* badly as a shopwindow; it has failed to serve peasant youth. Children's books and those for pre-school age groups have been *ideologically and artistically* inferior and technically unsatisfactory, lacking in visual appeal, etc. This all stems from poor ideological leadership and editing, feeble educative and organisational work with authors and artists, and an almost total lack of connection with proletarian, *Komsomól*, pedagogic and youth communities. In other words, it has not met the requirements of the Party decision of August 1931.

A series of requests are therefore made to *Molodáya Gvárdiya*. We shall cite the first of these in full in order to convey something of the flavour, and give the gist of the others: 'To publish a number of volumes and series organising *Komsomól*, worker and peasant youth under the militant banner of bolshevism, educating them in a spirit of Leninist intolerance of all petty-bourgeois stumbling and deviations from the general Party line, and merciless struggle with ideologies inimicable from a class point of view to the proletariat, and with counter-revolutionary Trotskyism and vile liberalism.' (*1*)

A series of works on the history of the Party, etc., linking their themes with current problems, must be oriented on the generation just entering productive labour (2), and: '...To reflect, in artistic literature, the heroism of the building of socialism, the role of youth in it, the transformation of social relations and of the new men – the heroes of socialist construction...' (3).

Technical series were to be created at once, together with books designed to draw *Pioneers*[82] into social activities, etc. (4). The faults previously indicated – dryness and so on – must be eradicated (5).

Then follows a new reference to the role of the fellow-travellers, the last before they, like all the others, became 'Soviet' writers or ceased to be writers at all. The reference is remarkable in that it does not suggest the slightest change of policy toward them: 'The participation of major authors and artists must be enlisted in the creation of children's books.[83] While attracting proletarian writers into the creation of children's books, it is essential at the same time to maintain considerate relations with fellow-traveller writers and artists aspiring to create Soviet children's books, drawing them into this work and guaranteeing them political consultation and informed and comradely criticism.'

Various organisational measures, on which we need not dwell, are listed. We need perhaps note only their drastic nature, involving minute supervision by the Central Committee. And in a paragraph describing the desired nature of children's literature we have yet another indication of the elements of *naródnost'* – stimulation of the artistic potential of the child, with *partiinost'* – the promotion of the Party's viewpoint, via *idéinost'* – explanation and presentation of current policies: 'Children's literature must be militantly bolshevik, a call to struggle and to victory. The children's books must portray the socialist transformation of the country and the people in bright and imaginative forms, bringing up the children in the spirit of proletarian internationalism. While radically improving the presentation of children's books and illustrations, care must be taken that this does not lead to misinterpretation of the political object of the books or distortion of the aim of the artistic education of the children.'

In fact, as the RAPP leaders continued to develop their 'dialectical materialist artistic method', the Party's own policy had gelled into a coherent and communicable whole.

We need not rehearse all the ingredients yet again. The Communist Party's attitude to the artist, the politician's relationship with the writer, was by 1931 quite clear. Indeed in broad terms it had been clear for some ten years, and no brief formula could have been more expressive than that which occurred in a draft report in 1921 and which we chose to introduce this book:[84] 'Agitation and propaganda acquire special edge and efficacy when decked in the attractive and powerful forms of art...' There remained only to formalise and institutionalise this relationship and control its future development.

The society of 1931 was vastly different from that of 1921; in the space of one decade the Party had halted the retreat that was NEP and in its drive to create heavy industry and collectivise the land it was now very much on the offensive.[85] With the end of NEP (1928) came the end of overt opposition to the regime, and the time for equivocation was past. Those intellectuals who, in the early twenties had lived in daily expectation of the collapse of the Bolsheviks had now bitterly to acknowledge their disillusion. Those who had stood uncommitted on the sidelines were finding such a stance increasingly uncomfortable. 'Friend or foe?' and 'Those who are not with us are against us' became cries that were no longer to be ignored; the time had come when each writer had either to cast his lot with the Party or master 'the genre of silence'.[86] For more than a decade the Party had urged its aspiring young artists to learn from the 'specialists' it had so assiduously wooed, but now a whole new generation that had served this apprenticeship was entering the field. Though their gifts were uneven and limited, as the quality of writing in the thirties was soon to demonstrate, they no longer needed to defer quite so tactfully to their elders. However, this did not imply that they had automatically to subscribe to the principles laid down by RAPP. All the Party demanded of the writer, whatever his origin, was that he support its programme and be ready to dedicate his art to that end. The need was for some broad framework in which all such sympathetic writers could work together in harmony.

In the political leadership, too, the changes which we earlier suggested were necessary if the theories elaborated by the pre-revolutionary bolshevik intellectuals were ever to be translated into practice were now coming about. The 'steel' had been 'tempered'[87] in the Civil War and its aftermath and was now cutting through to the surface of the party apparatus, and successive cohorts from the party schools were challenging not only the non-party men but their own 'fathers', too. Zhdánov's words at the 1934 Congress of Writers were to sum up their programme quite succinctly: '... the Party is organising the masses for the struggle to destroy capitalist elements once and for all, to eradicate the vestiges of capitalism in our economy and *in people's minds*.'[88] It was in this last connection,

clearly, that the writer as the engineer of the human soul was to be en-
rolled to play his part.

In such circumstances, some formalisation of policy toward the arts
seemed inescapable. Nor was the form it took an occasion for surprise. The
Party had always looked to the proletarian writer to earn his 'hegemony',
and despite its multiplying differences with the RAPP leadership,[89] its
natural allies and strength lay in the RAPP members, many of whom
had long since been out of sympathy with Averbákh's policies. By 1932
the differences were in any case perhaps more on the level of explicit
policies than of implicit goals, and if the Party was to extend its now
fully worked-out policy to embrace the entire intellectual stratum, then
RAPP as an exclusive organisation had to go, though much of its philosophy would remain.

The final party statement on our list, the 1932 Central Committee decision 'On the Reformation of Literary-Artistic Organisations' (*Appendix
V*) was brief and very much to the point, and seems to have been greeted
with some enthusiasm (if limited comprehension) by most of the writers
of the time. Apart from its refreshing brevity, it is very reminiscent in
tone of the 1925 statement.

The position that had obtained in the early 1920s, the Central Committee
said, had now been reversed: proletarian literature was strong and 'alien'
elements weak. But the existing proletarian organisations were too restrictive for the new circumstances; they were therefore to be abolished
and replaced by one single union – for each branch of the arts, but beginning with literature – which would accommodate 'all writers supporting
the platform of Soviet power and aspiring to take part in the building of
socialism,' and would include a communist fraction. VOAPP and RAPP
were therefore dissolved.

Dissolved, too, though this was not stated, were all the other artists'
associations, since any artist who supported the regime could do so via the
new union. He need not, of course, become a member of the Party;[90] indeed, a high proportion of the members of the Writers' Union are not
party members even today. But he could not overtly express dissent
without running the risk of being accused of a criminal offence – as
was to be the case in more recent times with Sinyávsky[91] and Daniél –
since it was expressly forbidden by law to issue, publish or distribute any
works containing 'agitation and propaganda against the Soviet regime
and the dictatorship of the proletariat' – terms capable of widely different
interpretations. Enforcement of this ruling is part of the wider function
of the Chief Administration for the Preservation of State Secrets in the

Press (*Glavlit*),[92] which dates in its present form from June 1931, though its origin goes back to 1922, a time when the new republic felt itself isolated and threatened on all sides by very real dangers.

The decision to reorganise RAPP and the other associations was followed by a period of intense organisational activity, since all the details had still to be worked out. In order to prepare the formation of the newly decreed Union of Soviet Writers (like the Federation already discussed, it does not mention the term 'proletarian' in its title), a fifty-man All-Union Organising Committee was set up and this began work in August 1932 with Górky as President, Grónsky as Chairman and Kirpótkin as Secretary. To Grónsky is ascribed, in one variant, the first use of the term 'socialist realism'.[93]

The term, whoever first used it, was adopted to designate the 'artistic method' proclaimed by Górky and Zhdánov at the first Congress of Soviet Writers in 1934, marking the foundation of the Writers' Union. In our final chapter we shall examine the analysis of the method given in 'Basis of Marxist-Leninist Aesthetics' (*Osnóvy markslstsko-léninskoi estétiki*), together with certain significant commentaries on its development and the attitudes to it of past and present leaders of the Communist Party.

4   Socialist Realism

'...Of course there must be some external resemblance in the
features, the shape of the eyes, the colour of the hair and so forth.
But isn't it rash to believe that we can see and know reality exactly as
it is – particularly when it's a question of the spirit? Who can perceive the spirit? But if I look at the person whose portrait I am painting and discern potential qualities of mind or character which he
hasn't so far shown in life, why shouldn't I depict them? What's
wrong about helping a man to find his higher self?'
'That's pure Socialist Realism! ...'

Solzhenitsyn: *The First Circle*

WHEN considering Lénin's theses and the interpretation subsequently
put upon them we must be aware that we have to do with an evaluation
of nineteenth century phenomena from a twentieth century point of view;
we are all the time arguing from hindsight. This is not of itself pernicious;
every generation of historians interprets the past afresh in the light of its
own experience, and in the process it is more than likely that one kind of
distortion is thereby substituted for or overlaid with another. The *klássovost'* of the artist's comprehension of 'reality' is matched by that of the
historian. As Lénin latched upon the positive, 'popular' aspects of Hérzen,
Belínsky, Chernyshévsky and Dobrolyúbov, so his heirs and successors
chose to stress those aspects of Lénin's thinking that fit their own thesis.
The ideologist is imprisoned in his ideology.

So it is with the theory of Socialist Realism, which we earlier stated
to have been formulated largely in retrospect. This is an important
factor, perhaps too often neglected. Far from being a new system foisted
on the cowed and unwilling artist (though uncomprehending, he may
most certainly have been), it was in fact an interpretation, within the
context of Marxist-Leninist ideology, of artistic developments throughout
the proletarian period of the revolutionary movement. It was an attempt
to codify those developments and project them into the future, transforming the artist's 'tendency' into a conscious programme. The developments themselves were not peculiar to Russia, so that a further essential

step towards our understanding is to regard Socialist Realism, at least in
the first instance, on a rather broader backcloth than that of the Soviet
Union alone.

*   *   *

I

Socialist Realism is a world-wide artistic phenomenon that arose under the
influences of the great social changes at the end of the nineteenth century
and the beginning of the twentieth – the sharpening contradictions within
capitalist society, the crisis in bourgeois culture and the rise of a socially
conscious proletariat. It is therefore the reflection in the arts of the struggle
for the victory of socialism [1].

In Russia, it developed during the third, proletarian, period of the
revolutionary movement and is still developing. In literature it traces its
antecedents to Púshkin and Tolstóy; in painting to Répin and Súrikov;
in music to Glínka and Músorgsky; in the theatre to Vólkov and Shchép-
kin; in architecture to Kazakóv and Bazhénov, and in criticism and aesthetics to Hérzen, Belínsky, Chernyshévsky and Dobrolyúbov.

As in Chapter 1 the ensuing summaries of specifically Soviet argument
are distinguished by being set in smaller print, with an asterisk preceding
each relevant paragraph.

*From the 1880s–1890s, the deepening crisis in bourgeois-capitalist
society led to the decline of realism and the rise of modernist schools –
futurism, cubism, expressionism, dadaism, surrealism, etc. – all of which
meant a widening of the gap between art and the masses. At the same time,
the realist tradition of the nineteenth century was continued and developed,
in the West by such writers as Anatole France and Bernard Shaw, and in
Russia by such exponents as Búnin and Kuprín in literature, Seróv in painting, Rakhmáninov in music and Stanislávsky in the theatre.

* The accession of the Bolsheviks to power in 1917 led to a radical change,
foreshadowing the end of the divorce of art from the people and hence of
'formalism' in the arts. The new social system created unprecedented oppor-
tunities for the development of progressive art; *klássovost'* and *naródnost'*
began to merge. But this could not be accomplished overnight; therefore the
twenties saw the clash of the new realism with the formalist schools.

* Art, at the time of the October Revolution, was a weapon of capitalism;
the problem was to transform it into a weapon of socialism. In their attempts
to close the gap between themselves and the masses, artists followed a variety
of strange and contradictory paths, all on a background of savage class war.
During the period of the ascendancy of the bourgeoisie, formalism dominated
the arts, but as the proletariat gradually came to establish its position in the
socio-political sphere, so realism became re-established. But this was not the

critical realism of the nineteenth century; it was Socialist Realism.
* Even so, the realism of many of the artists of the time still bore the
imprint of modernism. Some began to look for guidance to the realists of the
second revolutionary period; in the theatre the slogan 'back to Ostróvsky' was
proclaimed; painters began to study the techniques of the *peredvízhniki*,
and architects began again to betray influences of Renaissance styles. Other
artists naturally continued nineteenth century traditions – Alekséy Tolstóy
in literature, Nésterov in painting and Stanislávsky in the theatre. Still
others contrived to combine realism with innovation without such a direct
link with the past – Mayakóvsky in poetry and Deinéka in painting (*see*
Plate IV). And even such formalists as Meyerkhóld and the the young Eren-
búrg found their work enriched by elements of realism.

* A series of factors contributed to the rise of the new realism: the artists'
desire to draw closer to the people; their wish to base their work on the solid
foundations of the classics, especially the democratic traditions of their nineteenth century predecessors; their desire to expunge elements of modernism
from their work and, above all, the infusion of communist ideology.

* A number of works now considered socialist-realist had appeared before
the invention of the name and promulgation of the method in 1932–4. These
included Górky's writings, Mayakóvsky's poems, Parts I and II of Shólokhov's *Quiet Don* (*Tíkhy Don*, 1928), Fúrmanov's *Chapáyev* (1923), Fadéyev's
The Rout (*Razgróm*, 1925–6), Vsévolod Ivánov's *Partisan Tales* (*Partizány*,
1921), Serafimóvich's *Iron Torrent* (*Zhelézny potók*, 1924), the production of
Trenëv's *Lyubóv Yarováya* at the Maly Theatre and Vsévolod Ivánov's
Armoured Train 14–69 (*Bronepóyezd 14–69*) at the Moscow Arts Theatre
(1927), and Eisenstein's film *Battleship Potëmkin* (*Bronenósets Potëmkin*,
1925).

* Outside the Soviet Union, elements of Socialist Realism may be seen in
the work of a whole variety of artists: Anatole France, Barbusse, Rolland,
Léger, Picasso, Neruda, Nezval, Amado, Hikmet, Andersen Nexö, Pratolini,
Gutuzzo, Bidstrup, Fučk, Guillén, Brecht, Becker, Eisler, Busch . . . The list
is well-nigh infinite.

2

The commonly alleged origin of the term 'Socialist Realism' is of some
interest, both anecdotal and in view of the importance sometimes attached
to it. Throughout the twenties and into the thirties various suggestions
had been made: *proletarian realism* (Gladkóv, Libedínsky), *tendentious
realism* (Mayakóvsky – an informative suggestion!), *monumental
realism* (Alexéy Tolstóy), *communist realism* (Grónsky), and in October
1932, at a meeting of writers in Górky's flat, the subject again came up
for discussion. Stálin, who was also present, listened for a while and then
intervened. 'If the artist is going to depict our life correctly, he cannot
fail to observe and point out what is leading it towards socialism. So this
will be socialist art. It will be socialist realism.'[2]

All these suggestions are interesting for the light they throw on the ideological development of their authors. *Proletarian* realism clearly comes quite close to the crux of the matter but seems to imply the total exclusion of non-proletarian, academic art. In the twenties and early thirties especially, we have to do with the two streams of art that we discussed earlier – the new 'popular' art of an increasingly socially-conscious and educated proletariat and peasantry, on the one hand, and academic art drawing sometimes closer to the masses, and sometimes becoming once more estranged from them, on the other. In this context, *proletarian* realism has a rather limited, Proletkult ring, even though its supporters in RAPP did not all necessarily imply such a connotation. Even more limited is *monumental* realism, for though 'monumental art' was a common term hallowed by Lénin [3] it signified only one restricted aspect and would therefore not do; it was, perhaps, the clever suggestion of a newly converted, ideologically uncertain 'fellow-traveller'. *Tendentious* realism will clearly not do, at least if interpreted in the light of the distinction we have already drawn between *tendentiousness* and *partiinost'*; Mayakóvsky, as Lunachársky pointed out,[4] was ideologically immature. *Communist* realism, too, is imprecise; the terms 'communism' and 'socialism' were and still are loosely used, yet this is more than a mere verbal quibble. Certainly to speak of 'communist realism' at the turn of the century is hardly appropriate and destroys much of the argument that Socialist Realism is both world-wide and pre-dates the October Revolution.

Having digressed on this theme it might be as well at this point to go a little further toward a clarification of our terminology, especially as there has been considerable discussion of this factor in Western commentaries.[5] The argument is, then, that Socialist Realism was a *tendency* in the arts associated with the rise of the proletariat and beginning, in Russia, in the middle of the 1890s. Only after formulation and promulgation at the 1934 Congress of Writers did it become the officially sponsored *method*, first in literature and subsequently in the arts in general. *Soviet*, on the other hand, is a geographical term referring to art created within the confines of what is now called the USSR after the Bolshevik revolution of 1917. In this sense it is merely a handy label that avoids the imprecision, unfortunately not always understood, implicit in referring to, say, Soviet literature as 'Russian'.[6] From a Marxist-Leninist viewpoint many works of art created in the Soviet period are clearly not socialist, many not realist, some neither; in this category we must place a very large proportion of the art of the twenties and early thirties, together with works that have incurred official displeasure since 1934, including the

post-war *causes célèbres* – Pasternák's *Dóktor Zhivágo*, stories by Sinyávsky and Daniél, Solzhenítsyn's *Cancer Ward* (*Rákovy kórpus*), *The
First Circle* (*V krúge pérvom*), etc. Indeed, for most Soviet works it is
prudent to speak only of the socialist-realist *elements* within them.[7] And
finally, there are works created by Russian artists in emigration, which are
obviously neither Soviet nor socialist-realist, though they may not be
devoid of elements of socialism and realism.

3

'Realism' in this sense means art that sets out to present a comprehensive
reflection and interpretation of life from the point of view of social
relations; 'Socialist' means in accordance with the policy of the Communist Party. Socialist Realism is therefore based on a direct relationship
between the artist and the process of building a new society; it is art
coloured by the experience of the working class in its struggle to achieve
socialism.

* Socialist Realism embraces all kinds and genres of art, manifesting itself
in a form appropriate to each genre. It progresses with time, so that the
Socialist Realism of the thirties no longer obtains; and it varies according to
country, so that Soviet Socialist Realism cannot simply be transplanted elsewhere. For literature, it is defined in the Constitution of the Union of Writers
of the USSR as set out in the proceedings of the First All-Union Congress
of Soviet Writers in 1934: 'Socialist Realism demands from the author a true
and historically concrete depiction of reality in its revolutionary development.
Moreover this true and historically concrete artistic depiction of reality must
be combined with the task of educating the workers in the spirit of Communism.'[8]

* For music it is similarly described, for instance in the Central Committee's message to the Second All-Union Congress of Composers in 1958:[9] 'The
method of Socialist Realism demands from Soviet composers a systematic
struggle with aesthetic over-refinement, lifeless individualism and formalism,
as well as with naturalistic primitiveness in art. Soviet musicians are called
upon to reflect reality in moving, beautiful, poetic images, permeated with
optimism and lofty humaneness, the pathos of construction and the spirit of
collectivism – all that distinguishes the Soviet people's perception of the
world.'[10]

* And for architecture the Central Committee's message to the Second All-
Union Congress of Architects in 1955 sets the tone: 'Developing and multiplying the best national traditions in the classical architecture of the peoples
of the USSR, Soviet architects ... must proceed from the demands of Socialist
Realism. Socialist Realism is incompatible with formalist techniques, blind
copying of architectural models of past epochs or negligent attitudes to the
architectural heritage. Simplicity, purity of form, attractive external appear-

ance and economy of design, attention to functional facilities – these are the
guiding characteristic features of Soviet architecture.'[11]

4

Such a formula takes account both of the broad principles of Socialist
Realism and of the specific features of the individual artistic genre. The
broad ideological-aesthetic principles are those of *naródnost'* and communist *idéinost'* (idea-ness) – that is, an organic link with the life of the
workers and the expression of the most advanced communist ideas. These
are conditioned by a number of other factors, such as the artist's ability
to apprehend what is progressive and new, his ability to perceive reality
with true historical optimism, his ability to combine innovation and the
development of the best classical traditions, and his determination to
express only the healthiest aesthetic tastes, rejecting all traces of formalism,
naturalism, etc.

* The relationship between art and reality is twofold: reality is reflected
in art, but art also exerts an active effect upon that reality. Socialist Realism
demands a profound and true perception of reality and reflection of its chief
and most progressive tendencies; but it is itself a powerful weapon for changing reality. In both content and form, it has the same fundamental aims – to
assist the people and the Communist Party to create a new society, a better
man and a more perfect world. The principles of true reflection of reality and
ideological education of the masses are aspects of the same thing, since
artistic truth facilitates the development of communist awareness, and education in the spirit of communism is possible only through a true reflection of
life. Therefore a true reflection of reality subsumes the expression of communist ideals.

* But the *idéinost'* of a work of art lies not simply in formal, explicit
declarations but in the means by which reality is revealed and interpreted.
Otherwise, the result is only dry illustrativeness, harmful to art and ineffec-
tual from the point of view of inspiration and education. (An example of the
interdependence of truth of perception and *idéinost'* is provided by Shólokhov's *Virgin Soil Upturned*: the profound significance of the transformation in rural life could be portrayed correctly only because of the author's
own ideological standpoint, and his analysis of rural life in its revolutionary
development naturally added strength to his own socialist ideals.)

* All works in all genres have in common the fact that they reflect some
basic aspect of the life of the people, but this is embodied in concrete forms
that correspond to the specific nature of those works and genres. The most
important socialist aspect is the forward-looking nature of art, since the
artist is armed with knowledge of what must happen in the future and works
through his art to bring it about.

* Socialist realist art must reflect and comment on the burning issues of the

day; therefore the most significant socialist-realist works of any epoch are those most 'historically concrete' in this sense of being concerned with such issues. Examples are Fadéyev's *The Rout* (1925–6), Alexéy Tolstóy's *Road to Calvary* (*Khozdéniye po múkam*, 1928–41), and *Peter the First* (*Pëtr Pérvyi*, 1945), Mayakóvsky's poems *It's Good* (*Khoroshó*, 1927) and *Vladímir Ilyích Lénin* (1924), Tvardóvsky's *Land of Murávia* (*Straná Muráviya*, 1934–6), the film trilogy about Maksím [12] and Johansón's painting *At an Old Urals Works* (*Na stárom ural'skom zavóde*, 1937, *see* Plate V).

Such works illustrate the true nature and spirit of Soviet art and culture.[13]

5

Socialist Realism does not present a set of mechanical rules for application in any work of art, but it does give an indication of the general line that is to be encouraged in given circumstances. One of its fundamental characteristics is a constant attempt to present a profound but up-to-date depiction of reality, but this must not be confused wih 'photographic' art or naturalism. Nor does the truth of an artistic image depend on the way in which it illustrates 'correct' propositions; art that is simply a compound of abstract ideas will not – however 'correct' the ideas may be – contain artistic truth.[14]

* The method necessitates *generalisation* and *typification*, since a work of art is realistic only if it combines true to life, concrete reflection of reality with penetration into the depths of its meaning. This accounts for the total incompatibility of Socialist Realism and formalism, socialist art and bourgeois art. Socialist Realism is the mainstream of artistic development; formalism is a blind alley. It is subjective, and since its reflection of reality is thus distorted, its artistic form is also misshapen. To the formalist there is no objective truth, only the artist's own self. Therefore formalism is a denial also of artistic truth. By divorcing art from reality, claiming the independ ence of art, it betrays its scorn of reality.[15] This does not mean that many formalist artists are not extremely talented, but by following the path of bourgeois individualism they ruin their art. What good art they create is achieved in spite of their modernism. There are certain formalists who work both in public life and through their art to forward the cause of the masses and give expression to progressive ideas, and this produces contradictions within their art. Picasso, for instance, produced works of great artistic merit on the one hand and purely formalist works on the other. The contradictions within such an artist's work may be severe, but they cannot obscure the fact that formalism is basically antipathetic to realism and to art itself, since it is a function of the crisis in bourgeois culture.

The precise extent of the antagonism between Socialist Realism and formalism may be brought out by an examination, in particular, of the specific features of artistic creation. A 'true and historically concrete depiction of reality' requires the artist to maintain the closest possible links with the masses. And since the artist must reveal the processes at work in society, he must therefore concern himself with the questions that are at any given moment troubling that society, that is, he must concern himself with topical questions. This demands a high degree of artistry, for he is continually called upon to create artistic images of social phenomena that are quite new. (It is by their ability to evolve an aesthetic in response to the enormous challenge presented by the socialist transformation of society after the Revolution that the greatness of Mayakóvsky and Górky may be judged.) By revealing the new features of society as it progresses toward Communism and by endorsing them, the artist assists the masses to understand them, support them and assimilate them into their social, moral and aesthetic attitudes. This all requires an art that is able to express wisdom and emotion and to accommodate large-scale characters of universal stature.

6

An important element in revolutionary activity is *revolutionary romanticism*, and this too must find its place in socialist art. In fact Socialist Realism embodies the 'pathos' of the creation of a new society and of the vision that urges people on. This is not idle dreaming but a vision of the future based on an understanding of reality and the processes of development.[16] Such a fusion of realist portrayal of life with revolutionary romanticism is one of the most important innovatory features of the method.

* Clarity of purpose and an understanding of the processes of historical development and hence of the future enable the socialist realist artist to place his characters in concrete circumstances as men of the future in the society of the future.[17] This is the poetry of Soviet reality. It should not, of course, be identified with the sort of external decorativeness and rhetoric that characterised much of the art of the Stálin period, during which the function of art was simply to idolise one man. In the cinema, for example, it is not films such as *The Vow* (*Klyátva*) that should be taken as models, but *The Cranes Are Flying* (*Letyát zhuravlí*), *The Communist* (*Kommunist*), *A Man's Fate* (*Sud'bá chelovéka*), *Ballad of a Soldier* (*Balláda o soldáte*).[18]

* The problem of revealing the poetry of the revolutionary period introduces the question of positive and negative attributes, on which there has been considerable controversy as a result of a tendency on the part of some artists to adopt too mechanical an approach. The real question is not one of balancing the good and bad characters in a work, or of attributing negative features to a positive character in the interests of verisimilitude. For in an epoch which has broken with the past and embarked on an unprecedented programme of building a new future, the vital task is to discern the seeds of that future in the present. Although it is sometimes claimed that endowing a positive character with a certain minimal number of negative traits renders it more lifelike and convincing, the experience of Soviet art would suggest

otherwise. Neither Polezháyev, in the film *The Baltic Deputy* (*Deputát Báltiki*), for example, nor Shákhov in *The Great Citizen* (*Velíky grazhdanín*) [19] have any such negative traits, but they are lifelike and vivid. The characters are balanced and complete without any admixture of weaknesses to set off their strengths, for this would result not in verisimilitude but in illogicality.

* If art is to be true to life, what it requires is not a sort of mathematical calculation of good and bad features but a method of approaching reality. Socialist Realism is precisely such a method, and it demands that the artist be able to perceive the beauty and poetry of that reality. Plastóv's painting *The Tractormen's Dinner* (*Uzhin traktorístov*, 1951), *see* Plate VII, for example, is quite devoid of any artificial emphasis on the 'positive', but the artist's instinct and knowledge of reality enabled him to catch the genuine poetry of farm life in the 1950s.

* Speaking at the Third Writers' Congress in 1959, Mr Khrushchëv made an authoritative statement on this theme that is still valid. The Party, he said, 'is behind those writers ... who take positive phenomena as their basis and ... show the "pathos" of labour, setting men's hearts alight, urging them forward and pointing the path to a new world. In their positive heroes they somehow epitomise all the best characteristics and qualities of man and contrast them with negative images, demonstrating the struggle of the new against the old, and the inevitable victory of the new.' [20]

* This illustrates the didactic role of Socialist Realism, which is above all to provide a positive model drawn from real life. But this does not mean that the artist simply records the positive features or characters he observes in society around him; he must reveal them in their social significance as well as in their own individuality. So the importance lies not simply in the character whom the author portrays, but in what the author reveals by portraying that character. Without this, the result is banality.

* Many works, are indeed, banal; sometimes because the author lacks technical mastery, but usually because he in fact has nothing to say. No amount of rhetoric will conceal this banality; conversely, a work that conveys a broad and powerful depiction of reality cannot be marred by even the most daring hyperbole or invention.[21]

7

Since Socialist Realism is said to be an organic continuation and development of classical traditions, it is vital to clarify its precise relationship with the classical heritage. In principle this was determined, as we have seen, by Lénin, whose polemics with the Proletkult were mentioned in Chapter 1 and further discussed in Chapter 3. Lénin's attitude sprang from his analysis of the *naródnost'* of the nineteenth-century democrats (Chapter 2) but was also influenced by certain other extra-artistic factors. The current exposition takes the following form:

* At the time of the Revolution the cultural level of the masses was extremely low, since art was divorced from the mass of the people. Even the most 'popular' artists, such as Púshkin, Tolstóy, Répin, Súrikov, Músorgsky and Chaikóvsky, were known to only a tiny minority. On such soil it was impossible to cultivate an entirely new 'proletarian' art; the first step was to bring the best of classical traditions home to the people [22] and, indeed, to the artists. This did not imply slavish imitation or borrowing, but conscious assimilation and reworking: '... not the invention of a new, proletarian culture, but the *development* of the best models and traditions, the results of *existing* culture from the point of view of the Marxist outlook and the conditions of the life and struggle of the proletariat in the epoch of its dictatorship.' [23] In such a progression, Socialist Realism becomes a stage in the organic development of art throughout the ages, not a formalistic aberration. The 'great Communist art' of the future will provide hitherto unknown possibilities for the elaboration of new art forms, but these will arise on the basis of the distilled experience of progressive mankind throughout his entire history. It is these possibilities for development that give Socialist Realism its innovatory character.

* The most important innovatory feature of Socialist Realism is the fact that it participates actively and consciously in the building of a new society. The formation of aesthetic tastes is obviously influenced by a number of extra-artistic factors, such as working conditions, the level of technological development, the organisation of daily life, the material standard of living, the visible rate of improvement, general cultural level and so on. Moreover such factors also have a direct influence on intellectual and emotional attitudes; the men of the space age think differently from those who believed that thunder was the sound of Elijah's chariot. But these influences operate to integrate man in society – not, as bourgeois thinkers maintain – to isolate him from it. To the bourgeois, the age of the atom bomb is one of terror; to the Soviet citizen it is an age of pride in Man's achievements.

* In such a context, art is presented with a challenge more severe than ever before, and the problem of content and form becomes correspondingly acute. In the early days of the Soviet period, dogmatic attitudes to the classical heritage hindered response to the challenge, but the policy developed by the Party is not to consign classical principles and techniques to the archives but to learn from them and develop them further. Certain outstanding Soviet artists have already pointed the way: Fadéyev – from Tolstóy; Johansón – from Répin (*see* Plates II and V). At the same time, full rein must be given to the innovatory potential of Socialist Realism, and here we have notable examples in the way that Shostakóvich and Prokófyev have continued classical traditions and at the same time embraced new content and form. The socialist-realist attitude to the classics is therefore one of *critical analysis and development.*

8

Socialist-realist art must portray reality objectively and assist the masses to understand historical processes and their own role in them. It is thus one of the means of developing the social awareness of the people. Lénin highlighted this aspect of Górky's novel *The Mother* (*Mat'*, 1907);[24] it also explains the importance attached to artistic works from other countries, such as Aragon's *Les Communistes*.

* The role of the arts in this sense was redefined at the XXIst Congress of the Communist Party by Mr Khrushchëv:

> In the development and enrichment of the culture of socialist society, an important part is played by literature and the arts, which *actively facilitate the formation of the man of Communist society* ... There is no loftier or nobler task than that which stands before our art – *to record the heroic feats of the people*, that is building Communism. We call upon our writers, theatre and cinema workers, musicians, sculptors and painters to raise the ideological and artistic level of their works, to remain in the future *active helpers of the Party and government in the communist education of the workers, in propagandising the principles of communist morality, the development of a multi-national socialist culture and the formation of aesthetically good taste.** [25]

*One of the aims of the Communist Party is to develop the human personality to produce 'men who can do everything', and to this end it is conducting broadly educational activities on a very wide scale; the *educative role* of Socialist Realism can be understood properly only within the context of this work as a whole. Moreover communist education should not be considered as concerned only with ideology: it includes the raising of productivity on the basis of improved technology, shortening the working day, communist methods of labour organisation, raising the material standards of the masses, enlisting public opinion in the drive for better health standards and more harmonious communal living, the development of general and specialist education, and the all-round stimulation of initiative by the masses in all spheres of the economic, communal and public life of the country. In all this, an enormous role is played by various propaganda techniques, especially directed towards improving mastery of Marxist-Leninist theory, and by all the cultural forces – not the least amongst these being art.

* But art, of course, cannot function divorced from life. It can play its part only when firmly rooted in the life of the society. The distinction between propagandist works, on the one hand, and works of art, on the other, is false if based on the assumption that universally significant works of art are not firmly linked with problems of real life: Sophocles' *Antigone*, Cervantes' *Don Quixote*, Tolstóy's *War and Peace* (*Voiná i mir*) and Górky's *The Mother* (*Mat'*) were all concerned with burning issues of the day.

* 'Educating the workers in the spirit of Communism' means using art to develop and stimulate the best qualities in Soviet man:

> The entire ideological effort of our Party and government is enlisted to develop the new qualities of Soviet man, to educate him in the spirit of collectivism and love of work, socialist internationalism and patriotism, the high moral principles of the new society and the spirit

of Marxism-Leninism ... We must develop in Soviet man our communist morality, at the root of which is dedication to Communism and irreconcilable hostility to its enemies; acknowledgement of social obligations; active participation in working for the common good; voluntary conformity with the basic rules of communal living; comradely mutual aid, honesty, justice and intolerance of infringements of social order.[26]

* This catalogue of desirable qualities is in fact a programme for the artist, whose 'true and historically concrete depiction of reality in its revolutionary development' is inseparably bound up with communist *idéinost'*. Art cannot flourish in isolation, and whereas the Communist Party does not dictate what the author must write about, if he is in tune with society he cannot help being concerned with the same issues as are occupying the attention of the Party. But he can understand these issues correctly only via *partiinost'*: the *idéinost'* of his work is revealed in his choice of topic; his *partiinost'* – in the point of view from which that topic is perceived.

9

The *originality* of the artist's work lies in the way in which he expresses his own individuality, but this does not result from a conscious attempt to be different by cutting himself off from reality. If he is partisan and genuinely gripped by the 'pathos' of his subject, the artist will perceive it correctly and consequently be able to embody his perception in a genuine and original work of art, but this is quite different from merely indulging a subjective whim.

* As society evolves and becomes more complex, so the educative role of art as a form of social consciousness also develops. Art does not set out to train specialists in a narrow sense, but it must become what Chernyshévsky called a 'textbook of life', from which men may learn how to live together. Socialist Realism has an enormous educative role in teaching people to live in a communist society. This is at the root of its irreconcilable hostility to any degree of formalism, i.e. of subjectivism, which denies the social and educative function of art.

* The proper vehicle for the artist's subjectivity is his manner of expression. But effective participation in the socio-political sphere is possible only from the correct socio-aesthetic standpoint. Though art cannot be effective unless it is artistically convincing, mastery is not simply a question of technique. It is concerned above all with content.

* Genuine art is striking by virtue of the wealth of ideas and emotions it conveys, whereas inferior art merely degrades what may be a lofty theme. Hence the importance of the subjective element in art. Eloquence and expressiveness are not achieved simply by the application of formalist techniques; they are a direct function of the writer's involvement in his theme. But the expression of ideas and emotions nevertheless demands constant attention to matters of artistry, and the expression of the socialist-realist perception of reality similarly requires the constant development of artistic

genres, styles and techniques. Within the limits of its general principles and objectives, Socialist Realism stimulates free development of individual styles. By its very nature, art has to do with the infinite variety of man's relationships with the world around him, and to encompass this enormously wide and complex material it gives rise to a similarly wide range of approaches. Therefore the range of styles does not result from the personal whims of the artists but from the nature of the subject matter, with all its wealth and variety of perceptions of reality. The difference between Stanislávsky and Vakhtángov, for instance, resulted not from their allegiance to different 'schools' but from the fact that they perceived and expressed different aspects of reality.

* In the final analysis, every aesthetic ideal is socio-aesthetic. For the Marxist-Leninist, beauty lies in human relationships shorn of any element of exploitation. The subject matter of Socialist Realism is the whole of life, but beauty is perceived from the point of view of Marxist-Leninist aesthetics. Everything that furthers the cause of the building of communism is beautiful.

* This provides a clear and unequivocal yardstick of beauty from the aesthetic, moral and political points of view. And a natural concomitant is a hatred of all forms of social evil, from the class enemy, on the one hand, to bureaucracy and insensitivity on the other. All such evils, the 'survivals of capitalism', must be unmasked and condemned.

10

The object of Soviet policy toward the arts has been to close the gap that lay between art and the masses, attacking this problem from the twofold standpoint as outlined by Lénin, bringing art to the people, and the people to art.

* Art has been brought to the people by massive publishing measures, the spread of cinema networks, establishing of theatres and orchestras, increased numbers of museums, exhibitions, picture galleries, etc.[27] – and closing the gap between the people and art is the subject of campaigns for the aesthetic education of the workers. The object is twofold, for not only must the cultural level of the masses be raised to the point at which they can appreciate works of art; the masses must themselves become actively involved in the process of artistic creation. To this end the Soviet authorities have developed, by a variety of direct and indirect means, a policy of encouraging participation in amateur artistic activities in clubs and comparable social institutions, and millions of people now take an active part.[28] However, this does not in the least imply that such activities leave no role for the professional artist. On the basis of the principles of Socialist Realism, amateur and professional art should contribute to a developing process of mutual enrichment.

* A tragic contradiction in pre-revolutionary society was that even those artists with a high element of *naródnost'* remained largely unknown to the majority of the people. The cultural revolution was directed at bringing both

the classics and contemporary art to the masses, and here the importance attached to Socialist Realism is that it defines the artist's educative role and helps him to fulfil it. The Soviet writer addresses the people on behalf of the people, not the elite on behalf of himself. If he ceases to reflect the real thoughts and aspirations of the masses and falls into the 'error' of subjectivism, this is inevitably reflected in his work, which therefore becomes unacceptable.

* To the socialist-realist writer, the people is the maker of history and the master of its own fate, responsible for the creation of all that is materially or spiritually valuable on earth. Therefore the subject of his writing is men, not problems.[29] Art devoted to problems of production or agriculture, with no revelation of human character at its heart, cannot effectively fulfil its function in society.[30] This is not to say that individuals take precedence over social considerations, for the individual is a part of the collective, and his personal interests are the same as those of the collective as a whole. Moreover by revealing the relationship between the individual and the collective (class, Party, mass), the socialist-realist has a greater scope for profound characterisation than the pre-Marxist critical realist had. In the same way, the socialist-realist, with his understanding of the processes of historical development, has greater possibilities for portraying the historic role of the people as a whole.

II

An enormously important though frequently neglected aspect of socialist-realist art is the fact of its multi-national nature, even within the USSR. We have already pointed out the unwisdom of equating the term 'Soviet' with 'Russian', forgetting that the Russian republic – though by far the largest in terms of area, population and power – is nevertheless only one of a number, and the Russian language only one of more than a hundred spoken and used as vehicles for artistic expression. We have seen in our previous chapter how the problem of the national (non-Russian) cultures received great attention in Party deliberations during the first crucial decade after the Revolution. In general, national cultures have been deliberately stimulated throughout the Soviet period under the slogan 'national in form, socialist in content'.

The *naródnost'* of the national form springs from the maintenance of a direct link with the people and should be clearly distinguished from *cosmopolitanism*[31] which, in Soviet parlance denotes the rootlessness consequent on the severance of such a link. Though the art of all the peoples of the USSR must be socialist, the art of each people retains its national flavour by virtue of its 'popular' origin. The *naródnost'* of the content of national cultures lies in their *idéinost'* and this is what unites them with Russian culture in Soviet culture. 'Bourgeois nationalism', which relates not only to form but to content, militates against proletarian internationalism and is therefore inimicable to Socialist Realism.

The year 1972 marked the fiftieth anniversary of the formation of the USSR after the uncertainties following the Revolution and Civil War. This was designated the occasion for deeper analysis of the multi-national aspects of Soviet culture and art within the USSR and also of the relationship between Soviet art and progressive art throughout the world. Visions of 'permanent revolution' were, as we have seen, shattered in the early days of the Soviet regime, but this is no longer the era of 'Socialism in One Country'; the Soviet Union now stands at the head of a whole group of people's democracies, each in its way committed to the building of socialism according to Marxist-Leninist principles. In such circumstances the Soviet writer is exhorted and enabled to look beyond the broad frontiers of Soviet culture to an even wider, emergent socialist art.

* * *

All the principles of Socialist Realism discussed above stem directly from the Marxist-Leninist understanding of the process of historical development, and the overriding factor is the role of the Communist Party as the bearer of that understanding. Through the principle of *partiinost'* the artist must, in fact, acknowledge the wisdom of the Party and its right to command his allegiance to its policy. The policy is put forward in positive terms, presenting an appeal and a challenge, but it does, of course, have a negative, prohibitory obverse – censorship. The vexed question of artistic freedom is interpreted, as we have seen, in the light of the extrapolated significance of Lénin's 1905 article. This was restated after Stálin's death in the Party's message to the Second Writers' Congress in 1954:

> In their creative work, Soviet writers receive their inspiration from the great ideals of the struggle for Communism and genuine freedom and happiness for the masses against all oppression and exploitation of man by man. To the false and hypocritical bourgeois slogan of the 'independence' of literature from society, and the false concept of 'art for art's sake', our writers proudly contrast their noble ideological stance of service of the interests of the masses, of the people.[32]

And in his Report of the Central Committee in March 1971, Mr Brézhnev gave explicit evidence that despite the so-called 'thaw', 'de-Stalinisation' and a degree of international detente, the change had been simply one of politicians, not of their relationship with the artists.

Having noted earlier in the report that 'our Soviet intelligentsia sees its mission in devoting its creative energy to the cause of the people, to the cause of building a communist society' and countered ideological heresies with a sweeping; 'There is no freedom in general, just as there is no democracy in general. This is a class concept', he moved on to discuss the 'moulding of the new man', which was one of the Party's main tasks. 'Communism', he said, 'is inconceivable without a high level of culture, education, sense of civic duty and inner maturity ...' and 'the moral and political make-up of Soviet people is moulded ... above all, by purposeful, persevering ideological and educational work by the Party, by all its organisations.' This echo of Lénin's 1905 article is later made a major theme:

> ... with our society's advance along the road of communist construction a growing role in moulding the outlook, moral convictions and spiritual culture of Soviet people is played by literature and art. Quite naturally, therefore, *the Party continues, as it always has done, to devote much attention to the ideological content of our literature and art and to the role they play in society.** In line with the Leninist principle of partisanship (*partiinost'*) we believe that our task is to direct the development of all forms of creative art toward participation in the people's great cause of communist reconstruction.[33]

The Party noted with approval that there had been an 'indisputable growth of the ideological and political maturity' of the 'creative intelligentsia', which had produced a number of talented works in various genres, dealing with 'truly important problems' and managing to do so 'realistically, from party positions, without embellishment and without playing up shortcomings'. In other words, there had been no return to the 'varnishing of reality' of Stalinist days, nor yet too critical a view of Soviet reality after Khrushchëv. There had, however, been 'complicating factors of another order' which operated 'to belittle the significance' of the achievement of the Party and the people, 'apparently by dwelling on problems no longer real and reviving recently discredited phenomena'. This somewhat cryptic passage, doubtless referring to an obsession by some artists with the theme of labour camps and violations of 'socialist legality',[34] led to an oblique reference to Solzhenítsyn: 'Workers in literature and art are involved in one of the most crucial sectors of the ideological struggle. The Party and the people have never reconciled nor will ever reconcile themselves to attempts, no matter who makes them, to blunt our ideological weapon and cast a stain on our banner. If a writer slanders

Soviet reality and helps our ideological adversaries in their fight against socialism he deserves only one thing – public scorn.'

The ideological weapon, in this context, is Socialist Realism, on the basis of which the Party . . . 'is for an attentive attitude to creative quests, for the unfolding of the individuality of gifts and talents, for the diversity and wealth of forms and styles . . .' This, with an earlier concern for artistic standards, seems to show a desire on the part of the politicians to re-emphasise the positive aspects of their policy toward the arts and to return, at least in the inflections of their dicta, to the less virulent style of the twenties. Thus, 'it cannot be said that all is well in the realm of artistic creative work, particularly as regards quality. It would not be amiss here to note that we are still getting quite a few works that are shallow in content and inexpressive in form . . .' The artist has sometimes been too easily satisfied, having chosen to work on 'a good, topical theme' he has not done it justice because 'he has not put all his effort, his talent into it'. But in startling contrast to Zhdánov's vicious invective or the crude, peasant coarseness of Khrushchëv, Brézhnev remarked mildly that 'it seems to me we all have the right to expect workers in art to be more demanding of themselves and their colleagues . . .' [35]

The 'workers' should be kept up to the mark by the critics, who should have 'pursued the party line more vigorously'. But, and the tone is once more reminiscent of early party pronouncements, while adopting 'a more principled stand' the critic should nevertheless 'combine exactingness with tact and a solicitous attitude to the creators of works of art'.

Socialist Realism, then, remains the artistic method of the arts in the Soviet Union, and while evolving with 'reality in its revolutionary development' it has persisted impervious to erosion or assault from within or without. Brézhnev's report stated the Party's attitude to art with complete clarity: 'The strength of the Party's leadership lies in the ability to spark the artist with enthusiasm for the lofty mission of serving the people and turn him into an ardent participant in the remaking of society along communist lines.'

* * *

In our Introduction to this examination of the origins and principles of Socialist Realism we cited two antipathetic versions, that of the 'Leninist' origin and that of the 'Stalinist aberration' theory and we wondered which was the more convincing. The time has now come to draw our conclusions.

Ever since Khrushchëv made his much publicised 'secret' speech in

1956, denouncing Stálin's despotism and the 'cult of personality', this has provided a convenient loophole for all the uneasy, both inside and outside the Soviet Union, to explain away all the 'negative' features of Soviet 'reality'. This is certainly what happens in literary criticism, in which it is claimed that Stalinist literature was not an inevitable form of Socialist Realism but a distortion of it. Although it is from Lénin's 1905 article that the principle of *partiinost'* derives, the blame for what happened in the arts in the 1930s is attributable not to Lénin but to Stálin. This argument seems curiously illogical. If Socialist Realism has a Leninist origin, it does not follow that Stalinist literature was a distortion of it.

Perhaps Stálin really did corrupt and distort 'reality'; but whereas in another society he might have encountered much more outspoken opposition from the writers, in the USSR this could not happen because the writer's function is to support the Party, whatever it does. In such circumstances the Soviet writer: '... ceases to be an intellectual, a creator of ideas, and becomes a retailer of the ideas of others ... He no longer searches for truth; he begins with the truth as revealed in the pronouncements of party leaders ...' [36]

This is the basis of *partiinost'*, which lies at the heart of Socialist Realism. Opposition to the Party is unthinkable. The writer must support the Party and its leaders, and in proportion as one single leader becomes preeminent, so his reflection in the 'press' will grow, and the 'cult of personality' is born. It may have reached its most incredible proportions with relation to Stálin, but it was at least incipient with relation to Khrushchëv himself. It is a direct result of *partiinost'*.

The question therefore arises as to whether or not the principle of *partiinost'* is properly attributable to Lénin. Here it would seem that although Lénin was obviously not in 1905 writing of the circumstances, unforeseen and unforeseeable, of – say – 1925, his later writings and, in particular, his draft resolution on the Proletkult (1920)[37] are strong indications that the principle of *partiinost'* as later formulated would have met with his approval. Though Lénin disappeared comparatively early from the scene, his draft resolution set the tone and at no time during the twenties was any abrupt change of policy noticeable nor any obviously alien element introduced. On the contrary, there is ample evidence – as we have seen – that the policy that developed organically throughout the decade was a logical development of Lénin's ideas. It may well be that had he foreseen the precise outcome of this relentless elaboration of his thesis, he would himself have demurred, but this must be only speculation.[38] *Partiinost'* stems directly from Lénin's concept of the party, and though successive party leaders have dissociated themselves from Stálin's excesses, each has re-asserted the principle. It was Leninist *partíinost'* that made Stalinist art possible.

A rather different impression of the origins of Socialist Realism may certainly be gained – and this may explain the prevalence of a point of view contradictory to that given above – if we insist on divorcing a consideration of literature and art from the socio-political context in which they arise and if we ignore the place occupied by 'artistic literature' in the Soviet concept of the 'press'. If art is placed in the centre of the stage and the momentous social and political events of the period recede into a hazy background, then the fate of the modernist movements of the first quarter of the century must indeed seem arbitrary and cruel. From such a viewpoint the transition from the 'liberal' tones of the 1925 decision [39] to the peremptory finality of the 1932 decision [40] must indeed seem abrupt, and Socialist Realism must indeed seem 'alien and strange'.[41] But it seems to me that this is an unreal vision, more acceptable, perhaps, than harsh reality, but rather less fruitful if our aim is really to understand. Whether we approve or not is another matter.

Appendix I

V. I. Lénin : Party Organisation and Party Literature [1]

The new conditions for Social-Democratic work in Russia which have arisen since the October Revolution [2] have brought the question of party literature to the fore. The distinction between the illegal and the legal press, that melancholy heritage of the feudal, autocratic Russia, is beginning to disappear. It is not yet dead, by a long way. The hypocritical government of our Prime Minister is still running amuck, so much so that *Izvéstia Sovéta Rabóchikh Deputátov* [3] is printed 'illegally'; but apart from bringing disgrace on the government, apart from striking further moral blows at it, nothing comes of the stupid attempts to 'prohibit' that which the government is powerless to thwart.

So long as there was a distinction between the illegal and the legal press, the question of the party and non-party press was decided extremely simply and in an extremely false and abnormal way. The entire illegal press was a party press, being published by organisations and run by groups which in one way or another were linked with groups of practical party workers. The entire legal press was non-party – since parties were banned – but it 'gravitated' toward one party or another. Unnatural alliances, strange 'bed-fellows' and false cover-devices were inevitable. The forced reserve of those who wished to express party views merged with the immature thinking or mental cowardice of those who had not risen to these views and who were not, in effect, party people.

An accursed period of Aesopian language, literary bondage, slavish speech, and ideological serfdom! The proletariat has put an end to this foul atmosphere which stifled everything living and fresh in Russia. But so far the proletariat has won only half freedom for Russia.

The revolution is not yet completed. While tsarism is *no longer* strong enough to defeat the revolution, the revolution is *not yet* strong enough to defeat tsarism. And we are living in times when everywhere and in everything there operates this unnatural combination of open, forthright, direct and consistent party spirit with an underground, covert, 'diplomatic' and dodgy 'legality'. This unnatural combination makes itself felt even in our newspaper: for all Mr Guchkóv's [4] witticisms about Social-Democratic tyranny forbidding the publication of moderate liberal-bourgeois newspapers, the fact remains that *Proletáry*, [5] the Central Organ of the Russian Social-Democratic Labour Party, still remains outside the locked doors of *autocratic*, police-ridden Russia.

Be that as it may, the half-way revolution compels all of us to set to work at once organising the whole thing on new lines. Today literature, even that published 'legally', can be nine-tenths party literature. It must become party literature. In contradistinction to bourgeois customs, to the profit-making, commercialised bourgeois press, to bourgeois literary careerism and individualism, 'aristocratic anarchism' and drive for profit, the socialist proletariat must put forward the principle of *party literature*, must develop this principle and put it into practice as fully and completely as possible.

What is this principle of party literature? It is not simply that, for the socialist proletariat, literature cannot be a means of enriching individuals or groups; it cannot, in fact, be an individual undertaking independent of the common cause of the proletariat. Down with non-partisan writers! Down with literary supermen! Literature must become *part* of the common cause of the proletariat, 'a cog and screw' of one single great Social-Democratic mechanism set in motion by the entire politically-conscious vanguard of the entire working class. Literature must become a component of organised, planned and integrated Social-Democratic Party work.

'All comparisons are lame', says a German proverb. So is my comparison of literature with a cog, of a living movement with a mechanism. And I daresay there will even be hysterical intellectuals to raise a howl about such a comparison, which degrades, deadens, 'bureaucratises' the free battle of ideas, freedom of criticism, freedom of literary creation, etc., etc. Such outcries, in point of fact, would be nothing more than an expression of bourgeois-intellectual individualism. There is no question that literature is least of all subject to mechanical adjustment or levelling, to the rule of the majority over the minority. There is no question, either, that in this field greater scope must undoubtedly be allowed for personal initiative, individual inclination, thought and fantasy, form and content. All this is undeniable; but all this simply shows that the literary side of the proletarian party cause cannot be mechanically identified with its other sides. This, however, does not in the least refute the proposition, alien and strange to the bourgeoisie and bourgeois democracy, that literature must by all means and necessarily become an element of Social-Democratic Party work, inseparably bound up with the other elements. Newspapers must become the organs of the various party organisations, and their writers must by all means become members of these organisations. Publishing and distributing centres, bookshops and reading-rooms, libraries and similar establishments – must all be under party control. The organised socialist proletariat must keep an eye on all this work, supervise it in its entirety, and, from beginning to end, without any exception, infuse into it the life-stream of the living proletariat cause, thereby cutting the ground from under the old, semi-Oblómov, semi-shopkeeper Russian principle: the writer does the writing, the reader does the reading.

We are not suggesting, of course, that this transformation of literary work, which has been defiled by the Asiatic censorship and the European bourgeoisie, can be accomplished all at once. Far be it from us to advocate any kind of standardised system, or a solution by means of a few decrees. Cut-and-dried schemes are least of all applicable here. What is needed is that the whole of our Party, and the entire politically-conscious Social-Democratic proletariat throughout Russia, should become aware of this new problem, specify it clearly and everywhere set about solving it. Emerging from the captivity of the feudal censorship, we have no desire to become, and shall not become, prisoners of bourgeois-shopkeeper literary relations. We want to establish, and we shall establish, a free press, free not simply from the police, but also from capital, from careerism, and what is more, free from bourgeois-anarchist individualism.

These last words may sound paradoxical, or an affront to the reader. What! some intellectual, an ardent champion of liberty, may shout. What, you want to impose collective control on such a delicate, individual matter as literary work! You want workmen to decide questions of science, philosophy or aesthetics, by a majority of votes! You deny the absolute freedom of absolutely individual ideological work!

Calm yourselves, gentlemen! First of all, we are discussing party literature and its subordination to party control. Everyone is free to write and say whatever he likes, without any restrictions. But every voluntary association (including the party) is also free to expel members who use the name of the party to advocate anti-party views. Freedom of speech and the press must be complete. But then freedom of association must be complete too. I am bound to accord you, in the name of free speech, the full right to shout, lie and write to your heart's content. But you are bound to grant me, in the name of freedom of association, the right to enter into, or withdraw from, association with people advocating this or that view. The party is a voluntary association, which would inevitably break up, first ideologically and then physically, if it did not cleanse itself of people advocating anti-party views. And to define the borderline between party and anti-party there is the party programme, the party's resolutions on tactics and its rules and, lastly, the entire experience of international Social-Democracy, the voluntary international associations of the proletariat, which has constantly brought into its parties individual elements and trends not fully consistent, not completely Marxist and not altogether correct and which on the other hand, has constantly conducted periodical 'cleansings' of its ranks. So it will be with us too, supporters of bourgeois 'freedom of criticism', *within* the Party. We are now becoming a mass party all at once, changing abruptly to an open organisation, and it is inevitable that we shall be joined by many who are inconsistent (from the Marxist standpoint), perhaps we shall be joined by even some Christian elements, and even by some mystics. We have sound stomachs and we are rock-like Marxists. We shall digest these inconsistent elements. Freedom of thought and freedom of criticism within the Party will never make us forget about the freedom of organising people into those voluntary associations known as parties.

Secondly, we must say to you bourgeois individualists that your talk about absolute freedom is sheer hypocrisy. There can be no real and effective 'freedom' in a society based on the power of money, in a society in which the masses of working people live in poverty and the handful of rich live like parasites. Are you free in relation to your bourgeois publisher, Mr Writer, in relation to your bourgeois public, which demands that you provide it with pornography in novels and paintings, and prostitution as a 'supplement' to 'sacred' scenic art? This absolute freedom is a bourgeois or an anarchist phrase (since, as a world outlook, anarchism is bourgeois philosophy turned inside out). One cannot live in a society and be free from society. The freedom of the bourgeois writer, artist or actress is simply masked (or hypocritically masked) dependence on the money-bag, on corruption, on prostitution.

And we socialists expose this hypocrisy and rip off the false labels, not in order to arrive at a non-class literature and art (that will be possible only in a socialist extra-class society), but to contrast this hypocritically free literature, which is in reality linked to the bourgeoisie, with a really free one that will be *openly* linked to the proletariat.

It will be a free literature, because the idea of socialism and sympathy with the working people, and not greed or careerism, will bring ever new forces to its ranks. It will be a free literature, because it will serve, not some satiated heroine, not the bored 'upper ten thousand' suffering from fatty degeneration, but the millions and tens of millions of working people – the flower of the country, its strength and its future. It will be a free literature, enriching the last word in the revolutionary thought of mankind with the experience and living work of the socialist proletariat, bringing about permanent interaction between the experience of the past (scientific socialism, the completion of the development of socialism from its primitive, utopian forms) and the experience of the present (the present struggle of the worker comrades).

To work, then, comrades! We are faced with a new and difficult task. But it is a noble and grateful one – to organise a broad, multiform and varied literature inseparably linked with the Social-Democratic working-class movement. All Social-Democratic literature must become Party literature. Every newspaper, journal, publishing house, etc., must immediately set about reorganising its work, leading up to a situation in which it will, in one form or another, be integrated into one Party organisation or another. Only then will 'Social-Democratic' literature really become worthy of that name, only then will it be able to fulfil its duty and, even within the framework of bourgeois society, break out of bourgeois slavery and merge with the movement of the really advanced and thoroughly revolutionary class.

Nóvaya zhizn', No. 12
13 November 1905
Signed: *N. Lénin*

Collected Works,
Vol. 10, pp. 44–49

Appendix II

V. I. Lénin: In Memory of Hérzen [1]

One hundred years have elapsed since Hérzen's birth. The whole of liberal Russia is paying homage to him, studiously evading, however, the serious questions of socialism, and taking pains to conceal that which distinguished Hérzen, the *revolutionary* from a liberal. The Right-wing press, too, is commemorating the Hérzen centenary, falsely asserting that in his last years Hérzen renounced revolution. And in the orations on Hérzen that are made by the liberals and Narodniks abroad, phrase-mongering reigns supreme.

The working-class party should commemorate the Hérzen centenary, not for the sake of philistine glorification, but for the purpose of making clear its own tasks and ascertaining the place actually held in history by this writer who played a great part in paving the way for the Russian revolution.

Hérzen belonged to the generation of revolutionaries among the nobility and landlords of the first half of the last century. The nobility gave Russia the Biróns [2] and Arakchéyevs,[3] innumerable 'drunken officers, bullies, gamblers, heroes of fairs, masters of hounds, roisterers, floggers, pimps', as well as amiable Manílovs.[4] 'But', wrote Hérzen, 'among them developed the men of December 14,[5] a phalanx of heroes reared, like Romulus and Remus, on the milk of a wild beast... They were veritable titans, hammered out of pure steel from head to foot, comrades-in-arms who went deliberately to certain death in order to awaken the young generation to a new life and to purify the children born in an environment of tyranny and servility.' [6]

Hérzen was one of those children. The uprising of the Decembrists awakened and 'purified' him. In the feudal Russia of the forties of the nineteenth century, he rose to a height which placed him on a level with the greatest thinkers of his time. He assimilated Hegel's dialectics. He realised that it was 'the algebra of revolution'. He went further than Hegel, following Feuerbach to materialism. The first of his *Letters on the Study of Nature*, 'Empiricism and Idealism', written in 1844, reveals to us a thinker who even now stands head and shoulders above the multitude of modern empiricist natural scientists and the host of present-day idealist and semi-idealist philosophers. Hérzen came right up to dialectical materialism, and halted – before historical materialism.

It was this 'halt' that caused Hérzen's spiritual shipwreck after the defeat of the revolution of 1848. Hérzen had left Russia, and observed this revolution at close range. He was at that time a democrat, a revolutionary, a socialist. But his 'socialism' was one of the countless forms and varieties of bourgeois and petty-bourgeois socialism of the period of 1848, which were dealt their death-blow in the June days of that year. In point of fact, it was not socialism at all, but so many sentimental phrases, benevolent visions, which were the expression *at that time* of the revolutionary character of the bourgeois democrats, as well as of the proletariat, which had not yet freed itself from the influence of those democrats.

Hérzen's spiritual shipwreck, his deep scepticism and pessimism after 1848, was a shipwreck of the *bourgeois illusions* of socialism. Hérzen's spiritual drama was a product and reflection of that epoch in world history when the revolutionary character of the bourgeois democrats was *already* passing away (in Europe), while the revolutionary character of the socialist proletariat had *not yet* matured. This is something the Russian knights of liberal verbiage, who are now covering up their counter-revolutionary nature by florid phrases about Hérzen's scepticism, did not and could not understand. With these knights, who betrayed the Russian revolution of 1905, and have even forgotten to think of the great name of *revolutionary*, scepticism is a form of transition from democracy to liberalism, to that toadying, vile, foul and brutal liberalism which shot down the workers in 1848, restored the shattered thrones and applauded Napoleon III, and which Hérzen *cursed*, unable to understand its class nature.

With Hérzen, scepticism was a form of transition from the illusion of a bourgeois democracy that is 'above classes' to the grim, inexorable and invincible class struggle of the proletariat. The proof: the *Letters to an Old Comrade* – to Bakúnin – written by Hérzen in 1869, a year before his death. In them Hérzen breaks with the anarchist Bakúnin. True, Hérzen still sees the break as a mere disagreement on tactics and not as a gulf between the world outlook of the proletarian who is confident of the victory of his class and that of the petty bourgeois who has despaired of his salvation. True enough, in these letters as well, Hérzen repeats the old bourgeois-democratic phrases to the effect that socialism must preach 'a sermon addressed equally to workman and master, to farmer and townsman'. Nevertheless in breaking with Bakúnin, Hérzen turned his gaze, not to liberalism, but to the *International* – to the International led by Marx, to the International which had begun to 'rally the legions' of the proletariat, to unite 'the world of labour', which is 'abandoning the world of those who enjoy without working'.[7]

* * *

Failing as he did to understand the bourgeois-democratic character of the entire movement of 1848 and of all the forms of pre-Marxian socialism, Hérzen was still less able to understand the bourgeois nature of the Russian revolution. Hérzen is the founder of 'Russian' socialism, of 'Narodism'.[8] He saw 'socialism' in the emancipation of the peasants *with land*, in communal land tenure and in the peasant idea of 'the right to land'. He set forth his pet ideas on this subject an untold number of times.

Actually, there is *not a grain* of socialism in this doctrine of Hérzen's, as, indeed, in the whole of Russian Narodism, including the faded Narodism of the present-day Socialist-Revolutionaries.[9] Like the various forms of 'the socialism of 1848' in the West, this is the same sort of sentimental phrases, of benevolent visions, in which is expressed the *revolutionism* of the bourgeois peasant democracy in Russia. The more land the peasants would have received in 1861 and the less they would have had to pay for it, the more would the power of the feudal landlords have been undermined and the more rapidly, freely and widely would capitalism have developed in Russia. The idea of 'the right to land' and of 'equalised division of land' is nothing but a formulation of the revolutionary aspiration for equality cherished by the peasants who are fighting for the complete overthrow of the power of the landlords, for the complete abolition of landlordism.

This was fully proved by the revolution of 1905: on the one hand, the proletariat came out quite independently at the head of the revolutionary struggle, having founded the Social-Democratic Labour Party; on the other hand, the revolutionary peasants (the Trudoviks [10] and the Peasant Union [11]), who fought for every form of the abolition of landlordism even to 'the abolition of private landownership', fought precisely as proprietors, as small entrepreneurs.

Today, the controversy over the 'socialist nature' of the right to land, and so on, serves only to *obscure* and cover up the really important and serious historical question concerning the difference of *interests* of the liberal bourgeoisie and the revolutionary peasantry in the Russian *bourgeois* revolution; in other words, the question of the liberal and the democratic, the 'compromising' (monarchist) and the republican trends manifested in that revolution. This is exactly the question posed by Hérzen's *Kólokol*,[12] if we turn our attention to the essence of the matter and not to the words, if we investigate the class struggle as the basis of 'theories' and doctrines, and not vice versa.

Hérzen founded a free Russian press abroad, and that is the great service rendered by him. *Polyárnaya Zvezdá* [13] took up the tradition of the Decembrists. *Kólokol* (1857–67) championed the emancipation of the peasants with might and main. The slavish silence was broken.

But Hérzen came from a landlord, aristocratic milieu. He had left Russia in 1847; he had not seen the revolutionary people and could have no faith in it. Hence his liberal appeal to the 'upper ranks'. Hence his innumerable sugary letters in *Kólokol* addressed to Alexander II the Hangman, which today one cannot read without revulsion. Chernyshévsky, Dobrolyúbov and Sérno-Solovyévich,[14] who represented the new generation of revolutionary *raznochíntsy*, were a thousand times right when they reproached Hérzen for these departures from democracy *to* liberalism. However, it must be said in fairness to Hérzen that, much as he vacillated between democracy and liberalism, the democrat in him gained the upper hand nonetheless.

When Kavélin,[15] one of the most repulsive exponents of liberal servility – who at one time was enthusiastic about *Kólokol* precisely because of its *liberal* tendencies – rose in arms against a constitution, attacked revolutionary agitation, rose against 'violence' and appeals for it, and began to preach tolerance, Hérzen broke with that liberal sage. Hérzen turned upon Kavélin's 'meagre, absurd harmful pamphlet' written 'for the private guidance of a government pretending to be liberal'; he denounced Kavélin's 'sentimental political maxims' which represented 'the Russian people as cattle and the government as an embodiment of intelligence'. *Kólokol* printed an article entitled 'Epitaph', which lashed out against 'professors weaving the rotten cobweb of their supercilious paltry ideas, ex-professors, once open-hearted and subsequently embittered because they saw that the healthy youth could not sympathise with their scrofulous thinking'.[16] Kavélin at once recognised himself in this portrait.

When Chernyshévsky was arrested, the vile liberal Kavélin wrote: 'I see nothing shocking in the arrests... the revolutionary party considers all means fair to overthrow the government, and the latter defends itself by its own means.' As if in retort to this Cadet,[17] Hérzen wrote concerning Chernyshévsky's trial: 'And here are wretches, weed-like people, jellyfish, who say that we must not reprove the gang of robbers and scoundrels that is governing us.'[18]

When the liberal Turgénev wrote a private letter to Alexander II assuring him of his loyalty, and donated two gold pieces for the soldiers wounded during the suppression of the Polish insurrection, *Kólokol* wrote of 'the grey-haired Magdalen (of the masculine gender) who wrote to the tsar to tell him that she knew no sleep because she was tormented by the thought that the tsar was not aware of the repentance that had overcome her'.[19] And Turgénev at once recognised himself.

When the whole band of Russian liberals scurried away from Hérzen for his defence of Poland, when the whole of 'educated society' turned its back on *Kólokol*, Hérzen was not dismayed. He went on championing the freedom of Poland and lashing the suppressors, the butchers, the hangmen in the service of Alexander II. Hérzen saved the honour of Russian democracy. 'We have saved the honour of the Russian name,' he wrote to Turgénev, 'and for doing so we have suffered at the hands of the slavish majority.'[20]

When it was reported that a serf peasant had killed a landlord for attempting to dishonour the serf's betrothed, Hérzen commented in *Kólokol*: 'Well done!' When it was reported that army officers would be appointed to supervise the 'peacable' progress of 'emancipation', Hérzen wrote: 'The first wise colonel who with his unit joins the peasants instead of crushing them, will ascend the throne of the Romanovs.' When Colonel Reitern shot himself in Warsaw (1860) because he did not want to be a helper of hangmen, Hérzen wrote: 'If there is to be any shooting, the ones to be shot should be the generals who give orders to fire upon unarmed people.' When fifty peasants were massacred in Bezdna, and their leader, Antón Petróv, was executed (12 April, 1861), Hérzen wrote in *Kólokol*:

'If only my words could reach you, toiler and sufferer of the land of Russia!... How well I would teach you to despise your spiritual shepherds, placed over you by the St. Petersburg Synod and a German tsar... You hate the landlord, you hate the official, you fear them, and rightly so; but you still believe in the tsar and the bishop... do not believe them. The tsar is with them, and they are his men. It is him you now see – you, the father of a youth murdered in Bezdna, and you – the son of a father murdered in Pénza... Your shepherds are as ignorant as you and as poor... Such was another Anthony (not Bishop Anthony, but Antón of Bezdna) who suffered for you in Kazán... The dead bodies of your martyrs will not perform forty-eight miracles, and praying to them will not cure a toothache; but their living memory may produce one miracle – your emancipation.' [21]

This shows how infamously and vilely Hérzen is being slandered by our liberals entrenched in the slavish 'legal' press, who magnify Hérzen's weak points and say nothing about his strong points. It was not Hérzen's fault but his misfortune that he could not see the revolutionary people in Russia itself in the 1840s. When *in the sixties* he came to see the revolutionary people, he sided fearlessly with the revolutionary democracy against liberalism. He fought for a victory of the people over tsarism, not for a deal between the liberal bourgeoisie and the landlords' tsar. He raised aloft the banner of revolution.

*   *   *

In commemorating Hérzen, we clearly see the three generations, the three classes, that were active in the Russian revolution. At first it was the nobles and landlords, the Decembrists and Hérzen. These revolutionaries formed but a narrow group. They were very far removed from the people. But their effort was not in vain. The Decembrists awakened Hérzen. Hérzen began the work of revolutionary agitation.

This work was taken up, extended, strengthened, and tempered by the revolutionary *raznochíntsy* – from Chernyshévsky to the heroes of *Naródnaya Vólya*.[22] The range of fighters widened; their contact with the people became closer. 'The young helmsmen of the gathering storm' is what Hérzen called them. But it was not yet the storm itself.

The storm is the movement of the masses themselves. The proletariat, the only class that is thoroughly revolutionary, rose at the head of the masses and for the first time aroused millions of peasants to open revolutionary struggle. The first onslaught in this storm took place in 1905. The next is beginning to develop under our very eyes.

In commemorating Hérzen, the proletariat is learning from his example to appreciate the great importance of revolutionary theory. It is learning that selfless devotion to the revolution and revolutionary propaganda among the people are not wasted even if long decades divide the reaping from the harvest. It is learning to ascertain the role of the various classes in the Russian and in the international revolution. Enriched by these lessons, the proletariat will fight its way to a free alliance with the socialist workers of all lands, having crushed that loathsome monster, the tsarist monarchy, against which Hérzen was the first to raise the great banner of struggle by addressing his *free Russian word* to the masses.

Sotsiál Demokrát, No. 26,
8 May (25 April) 1912

Collected Works,
Vol. 18, pp. 25–31

Appendix III

(*Documents on the Proletkults*)

(1) V. I. Lénin: On Proletarian Culture [1]

WE SEE from *Izvéstia* of October 8 that, in his address to the Proletkult Congress, Comrade Lunachársky said things that were *diametrically opposite* to what he and I had agreed upon yesterday.

It is necessary that a draft resolution (of the Proletkult Congress) should be drawn up with the utmost urgency, and that it should be endorsed by the Central Committee, in time to have it put to the vote *at this very* session of the Proletkult. On behalf of the Central Committee it should be submitted not later than today, for endorsement both by the Collegium of the People's Commissariat of Education and by the Proletkult Congress, because the Congress is closing today.

DRAFT RESOLUTION

(1) All educational work in the Soviet Republic of workers and peasants, in the field of political education in general and in the field of art in particular, should be imbued with the spirit of the class struggle being waged by the proletariat for the successful achievement of the aims of its dictatorship, i.e., the overthrow of the bourgeoisie, the abolition of classes, and the elimination of all forms of exploitation of man by man.

(2) Hence, the proletariat, both through its vanguard – the Communist Party – and through the many types of proletarian organisations in general, should display the utmost activity and play the leading part in all the work of public education.

(3) All the experience of modern history and, particularly, the more than half-century-old revolutionary struggle of the proletariat of all countries since the appearance of the *Communist Manifesto* has unquestionably demonstrated that the Marxist world outlook is the only true expression of the interests, the viewpoint, and the culture of the revolutionary proletariat.

(4) Marxism has won its historic significance as the ideology of the revolutionary proletariat because, far from rejecting the most valuable achievements of the bourgeois epoch, it has, on the contrary, assimilated and refashioned everything of value in the more than two thousand years of the development of human thought and culture. Only further work on this basis and in this direction, inspired by the practical experience of the proletarian dictatorship as the final stage in the struggle against every form of exploitation, can be recognised as the development of a genuine proletarian culture.

(5) Adhering unswervingly to this stand of principle, the All-Russia Prolet-kult Congress rejects in the most resolute manner, as theoretically unsound and practically harmful, all attempts to invent one's own particular brand of culture, to remain isolated in self-contained organisations, to draw a line dividing the field of work of the People's Commissariat of Education and the Proletkult, or to set up a Proletkult 'autonomy' within establishments under the People's Commissariat of Education and so forth. On the contrary, the Con-gress enjoins all Proletkult organisations to fully consider themselves in duty bound to act as auxiliary bodies of the network of establishments under the People's Commissariat of Education, and to accomplish their tasks under the general guidance of the Soviet authorities (specifically, of the People's Com-missariat of Education) and of the Russian Communist Party, as part of the tasks of the proletarian dictatorship.

* * *

Comrade Lunachársky says that his words have been distorted. In that case this resolution is needed *all the more* urgently.

Written on 8 October 1920   *Collected Works,*
First published in 1926 in *Krásnaya Nov'*, No. 3   Vol. 31, pp. 316–17

(2) On the Proletkults (Letter from the Central Committee, R.C.P.) [2]

THE CENTRAL COMMITTEE of the Party and, at its direction, the Commu-nist fraction of the last All-Russia Congress of Proletkults has adopted the following resolution:

(1) At the basis of the mutual relationships between the Proletkult and the People's Commissariat of Education [3] there must be the closest approximation of the work of both organs, in accordance with the Resolution of the IXth Congress of the R.C.P.;

(2) The creative work of the Proletkult must form one of the components of the work of the People's Commissariat of Education, the organ that is bring-ing about the dictatorship of the proletariat in the cultural field;

(3) In accordance with this requirement, the central organ of the Proletkult, since it takes an active part in the politico-educational work of the People's Commissariat of Education, becomes a section of the People's Commissariat of Education, subordinate to it and guided in its work by the line dictated by the People's Commissariat of Education of the Russian Communist Party;

(4) Inter-relationship of local organs: the inter-relationship of Departments of Public Education (*narobraz*) and Political Education Committees (*politpros-vet*) with the Proletkults must be of the same order: local Proletkults become sub-sections within the Departments of Public Education and are guided in their work by the line laid down by the Provincial Committees (*gubkom*) of the R.C.P. for the Provincial Departments of Public Education;

(5) The Central Committee of the R.C.P. directs the People's Commissariat of Education to create and maintain conditions that will guarantee the prole-tarians the possibility of free creative work in their establishments.

The Central Committee of the Russian Communist Party considers it necessary to offer the following elucidation to comrades in the Proletkults, and to
leaders of local and Provincial Departments of Public Education and Party
organisations:

The Proletkult came into being before the October Revolution.[4] It was proclaimed an 'independent' workers' organisation, independent of the Ministry
of Public Education of the Kérensky period. The October Revolution changed
the perspectives. The Proletkults continued to be 'independent', but now this
was 'independence' of the Soviet regime. For this and a variety of other
reasons there was an influx into the Proletkults of elements socially alien to us
– petty bourgeois elements who sometimes actually gained control of the
direction of the Proletkults. The Futurists, decadents, adherents of idealist
philosophy hostile to Marxism, and simply drop-outs from the ranks of bourgeois publicism and philosophy somehow began to direct all the affairs of the
Proletkults.

Under the guise of 'proletarian culture' the workers were offered bourgeois
views in philosophy (Machism)[5] and in the cultural field absurd, perverted
tastes (Futurism) began to find favour.

Instead of assisting proletarian youth to study seriously and deepen its
communist approach to all the problems of life and art, certain artists and
philosophers who were essentially far-removed from Communism and hostile
to it proclaimed themselves genuinely proletarian, gained control of the
Proletkults and prevented the workers from setting off on the highroad of free
and really proletarian creativity. Under the guise of proletarian culture, certain groups and groupings of the intelligentsia thrust their own semi-bourgeois
philosophical 'systems' and inventions on the progressive workers. The same
anti-Marxist views that had blossomed so luxuriantly after the defeat of the
1905 Revolution and for several years (1907–12) occupied the minds of the
'social-democratic' intelligentsia, nourished during the years of reaction by
God-building[6] and various kinds of idealist philosophy – these same views in
disguised forms are now the subject of attempts by anti-Marxist groups of
intellectuals to find favour via the Proletkults.

If our Party has not up to now interfered in this matter, this may be explained only by the fact that it has been engaged in military affairs at the
fronts, and has not therefore always been able to devote the necessary attention
to these important questions. Now, when the Party is faced with the opportunity to tackle cultural-educational work more thoroughly, it must devote far
more attention to questions of public education in general and the Proletkults
in particular.

The same elements of the intelligentsia that attempted to smuggle in their
reactionary views under the guise of 'proletarian culture' are now mounting a
noisy campaign against the above-mentioned decision of the Central Committee. These elements are trying to represent the Central Committee's resolution
as a step that must result in a restriction of the workers' artistic creativity.
This, of course, is not so. The best labour elements in the Proletkults understand entirely what motives have been guiding the Central Committee of our
Party.

Not only does the Central Committee not wish to restrict the initiative of the worker intelligentsia in the field of artistic creativity, it wants, on the contrary, to create the most healthy and normal conditions for it and to give it the opportunity to be reflected fruitfully in the whole matter of artistic creativity. The Central Committee realises clearly that now that the war is drawing to an end interest in questions of artistic creativity and proletarian culture will grow more and more in the ranks of the workers. The Central Committee values and respects the progressive workers' desire to raise, in their turn, questions of the spiritually richer development of the personality, etc. The Party will do all it can to ensure that this matter really does fall into the hands of the worker intelligentsia, and that the workers' government will give the worker intelligentsia all it needs for this purpose.

From the draft instructions worked out by the People's Commissariat of Education and confirmed by the Central Committee of our Party, all interested comrades will see that complete autonomy of the reorganised workers' Proletkults in the field of artistic creativity is guaranteed. The Central Committee has given quite detailed directives on this point for action by the People's Commissariat. And the Central Committee will watch, and entrusts the Provincial Party Committees to watch, that there is no petty tutelage of the reorganised Proletkults.

At the same time, the Central Committee realises that in the field of the arts the same intellectual currents that have been exerting a disruptive influence in the Proletkults have made themselves felt up to now in the People's Commissariat of Education itself. The Central Committee will achieve the removal of these bourgeois currents from the People's Commissariat, too. The Central Committee has taken a special decision, according to which the Provincial Departments of Public Education, which by the new resolution will direct the work of the Proletkults, will be made up of men who have been closely vetted by the Party. In the coalescence of the Provincial Departments of Public Education with the Proletkults, the Central Committee sees a guarantee that the best proletarian elements hitherto united in the ranks of the Proletkults will now take the most active part in this work and therefore aid the Party in giving all the work of the People's Commissariat of Education a really proletarian character. The closest possible combination, amicable work in the ranks of our educational organisations, which must become in practice, not simply in words, the organs of a genuine, not contrived proletarian culture – these are the aims for which the Central Committee of our Party now enlists us.

Pravda, No. 270
1 December 1920

Appendix IV

On the Party's Policy in the Field of Literature[1] (Resolution of the Central Committee of the R.K.P.(b), 18 June 1925)

(1) The rise in the material welfare of the masses in recent times, together with the mental transformation produced by the Revolution, the strengthening of mass activities, the gigantic widening of outlook, etc., is leading to an enormous growth in cultural enquiry and demands. We have thus entered the zone of cultural revolution, which is a prerequisite for further movement towards a communist society.

(2) One part of this mass cultural growth is the growth of a new literature – in the first instance proletarian and peasant, beginning with forms that are embryonic but at the same time unprecedentedly wide in scope (worker correspondents, rural correspondents, wall-newspapers, etc.) and ending with ideologically aware artistic-literary products.

(3) On the other hand, the complicated nature of the economic process, the contemporaneous growth of contradictory and even directly hostile economic forms and the process of engenderment and consolidation of a new bourgeoisie evoked by this process; the inevitable, though at first unconscious attraction towards it of a part of the old and new intelligentsia; the chemical separation of more and more ideological agents of the bourgeoisie from the depths of society – all this cannot help revealing itself on the literary surface of social life, too.

(4) Thus, just as class warfare is not coming to an end in the country in general, so it is not coming to an end on the literary front either. In a class society there is not and cannot be neutral art, though the class nature of art in general and literature in particular is expressed in forms that are infinitely more varied than, for instance, in politics.

(5) However, it would be quite wrong to lose sight of the basic fact of our social life, namely, the fact of the capture of power by the working class – the existence of the dictatorship of the proletariat.

If before the seizure of power the proletarian party sparked off the class war and followed a policy of disintegrating society as a whole, then in the period of the dictatorship of the proletariat the question before the party is that of symbiosis with the peasantry and its gradual transformation; the question of how to allow a certain measure of cooperation with the bourgeoisie while gradually squeezing it out; the question of how to put the technical and other intelligentsia at the service of the Revolution and to win them over ideologically from the bourgeoisie.

Therefore although the class war is not coming to an end, it is changing its form, for before the seizure of power the proletariat aspired to destroy the society of the times, but in the period of its dictatorship it gives priority to 'peaceful organisational work'.

(6) Preserving, consolidating and always widening its leadership, the proletariat must occupy a similar position in a series of new sectors of the ideological front also. The process of the penetration of dialectical materialism into quite new fields (biology, psychology, the natural sciences in general) has clearly begun. The conquest of this position in the realm of literature must also sooner or later become a fact.

(7) However, it must be remembered that this task is infinitely more complicated than the other problems that the proletariat is now solving. For even within the limitations of a capitalist society the working class was able to prepare for victorious revolution, building up cadres of fighters and leaders and working out a magnificent ideological weapon for the political struggle, but it could not work out the problems of the natural sciences nor technical problems, nor – being a culturally oppressed class – could it elaborate its own literature, its own special art form, its own style. If the proletariat already has in its hands infallible criteria of socio-political content, it has not yet such definite answers to all the questions concerning artistic form.

(8) The above must determine the policy of the ruling party of the proletariat in the field of literature. The following questions are pertinent in the first instance: the inter-relationships between the proletarian writers, the peasant writers and the so-called 'fellow-travellers' and the rest; the Party's policy toward the proletarian writers themselves; questions of criticism; questions of style and form in literary works and the method of working out new art forms; and finally, questions of an organisational character.

(9) The inter-relationship between the various groupings of writers according to their social-class and social-group content is determined by our general policy. However, it must be borne in mind here that guidance in the field of literature belongs to the working class as a whole, with all its material and ideological resources. There is not yet a hegemony of proletarian writers, and the Party must assist those writers to earn their historic right to such hegemony. Peasant writers must be awarded a friendly welcome, and they must have the advantage of our unconditional support. The problem is to steer their growing cadres onto the rails of proletarian ideology, while in no way expunging from their work the peasant literary images that are an indispensable prerequisite for influencing the peasantry.

(10) As regards the 'fellow-travellers', it is essential to bear in mind: (1) the fact that they differ amongst themselves; (2) the significance of some of them as qualified 'specialists' in literary technique; (3) the degree of wavering in this stratum of writers. The general directive here must be one of a tactful and considerate attitude to them, i.e. an approach that will guarantee them conditions for as quick as possible a transfer of allegiance to the side of communist ideology. While weeding out the anti-proletarian and anti-revolutionary elements (which are now extremely insignificant) and combating the ideology of the new bourgeoisie which is now in the process of formation amongst a part of the 'fellow-travellers' of the *Changing Landmarks* [2] persuasion, the Party

must address itself to the interstitial ideological forms, patiently assisting these inevitably numerous forms to return to full health in the process of an increasingly close and comradely cooperation with the cultural forces of Communism.

(11) As regards the proletarian writers, the Party must take up the following position: assisting their growth in all ways and giving full support to them and their organisations, the Party must by all possible means forestall the appearance of communist boasting (*komchvánstvo*),[3] since this is a most pernicious phenomenon. Precisely because the Party sees in them the future ideological leaders of Soviet literature, it must combat in every way any flippant or negligent attitude toward the old cultural heritage or toward specialists in the artistry of words. Equally deserving of condemnation is the position of underestimating the very importance of the struggle for the ideological hegemony of the proletarian writers. Against *kapitulyánstvo*[4] on the one hand and communist boasting (*komchvánstvo*) on the other – this must be the Party's slogan. The Party must also combat attempts at pure hot-house 'proletarian' literature: a broad encompassing of phenomena in all their complexity; not being confined within the framework of the factory alone; becoming a literature that does not belong in a workshop but to the great fighting class that brings the millions of peasants in its train – these must provide the framework for the content of proletarian literature.

(12) the foregoing is what defines in general and *in toto* the task of *criticism*, which is one of the most important weapons of education in the hands of the Party. Without for one moment relinquishing a communist position or moving one iota from proletarian ideology in revealing the objective class significance of various literary works, communist criticism must struggle mercilessly against counter-revolutionary manifestations in literature, unmask the *Changing Landmarks* liberalism, etc., while at the same time showing the very greatest tact, caution and patience in relation to those literary strata that could and will join cause with the proletariat. In its everyday usage communist criticism must drop the tone of literary command. It will have deep educative significance only when it relies on the excellence of its *ideals*. Marxist criticism must decisively expel from its midst any pretentious, semi-literate and smug *komchvánstvo*. Marxist criticism must adopt the slogan of study, and it must reject all trashy writing and egocentricity from its own midst.

(13) While gaining a deep and unerring knowledge of the socio-class content of the literary streams, the Party can in no way bind itself in adherence to any one direction *in the sphere of artistic form*. Though supervising literature as a whole, the Party can as little support any *one* literary fraction (classifying such fractions according to their views on form and style) as it can decide by decree the question of the form of the family, though in general it undoubtedly supervises and must supervise the building of a new way of life. All this leads to the supposition that the style appropriate to the epoch will be created, but it will be created by other methods, and no decision of this question has yet been remarked. All attempts to bind the Party to one direction at the present phase of the cultural development of the country must be firmly rejected.

(14) Therefore the Party must pronounce in favour of free competition between the various groupings and streams in this sphere. Any other decision of

the question would be an official-bureaucratic pseudo-decision. Similarly unacceptable would be the passing of a decree or party decision awarding a *legal monopoly* in matters of literature and publishing to some group or literary organisation. While giving material and moral support to proletarian and the proletarian-peasant literature, aiding the 'fellow-travellers', etc., the Party cannot grant a monopoly to one group, even the one with the most proletarian ideological content, for this would mean, above all, the destruction of proletarian literature.

(15) The Party must completely eradicate attempts at crude and incompetent administrative meddling in literary affairs. The Party must take pains to make a careful selection of personnel for the institutions that supervise matters of the press, in order to ensure really correct, helpful and tactful guidance of our literature.

(16) The Party must point out to all people working in the field of literature the necessity for a correct demarcation of the functions of the critics and the writers. For the latter, the centre of gravity of their work must be transferred to literary production in the proper sense of the word, making use of the gigantic material of the contemporary scene. It is also essential to pay greater attention to the development of national literatures in the numerous republics and provinces of the Union.

The Party must underline the necessity for the creation of a literature aimed at a genuinely mass readership of workers and peasants. We must break more boldly and decisively with the traditions of literature for the gentry (*bárstvo*) and make use of all the technical achievements of the old masters to work out an appropriate form, intelligible *to the millions*.

Soviet literature and its future proletarian avant-garde will be able to fulfil their historic cultural mission only when they have solved this great problem.

Party Workers' Handbook,
VIth edition, pp. 349–52

Appendix V

ON THE REFORMATION OF LITERARY-ARTISTIC ORGANISATIONS
(Decision of the Central Committee, V.K.P. (b) [1] 23 April 1932)

THE CENTRAL COMMITTEE has concluded that on the basis of the significant success in the building of socialism in recent years there has been a great quantitative and qualitative growth of literature and art.

A few years ago, when in literature there was still an obviously significant influence of alien elements, which were especially lively in the early years of NEP, and the cadres of proletarian literature were still weak, the Party helped in all possible ways toward the creation and strengthening of special proletarian organisations in literature and art in order to consolidate the position of the proletarian writers and artists.

At the present time, when cadres have had time to develop in literature and art, and new writers and artists have come forward from the mills, factories and collective farms, the framework of the existing proletarian literary-artistic organisations (VOAPP, RAPP, RAPM,[2] etc.) appears to be too narrow and to restrict the serious scope of artistic creativity. This circumstance creates the danger of distorting these organisations, from means for the maximum mobilisation of Soviet writers and artists around the problems of building socialism into means of cultivating exclusiveness in closed circles, divorced from contemporary political problems and from a significant group of the writers and artists who sympathise with the building of socialism.

Hence the need for an appropriate reformation of literary-artistic organisations and a broadening of the basis of their work.

Consequently the Central Committee, VKP (b) resolves:

(1) to liquidate the association of proletarian writers (VOAPP, RAPP);
(2) to unite all writers supporting the platform of Soviet power and aspiring to participate in the building of socialism into one union of Soviet, socialist writers with a communist fraction in it;
(3) to carry out an analogous change with regard to the other forms of art;
(4) to entrust the *Orgbureau* to work out practical measures for the implementation of this decision.

Partiinoye stroitel'stvo,
1932, No. 9, p. 62

References and Notes

The bulk of sources consulted in the writing of this study were in Russian. I have therefore listed them in transliteration, using a system slightly different from that used in the body of the text. References to Lénin's articles are to the *Collected Works* unless otherwise stated. Since my object in Chapters 1, 2 and 4 has been to present the Soviet viewpoint, I have restricted myself as much as possible to references made by the Soviet critics in the works consulted, citing translated versions wherever possible so that the non-Russian speaking reader may check them for aptness. However, in the interests of brevity and clarity I have had to add various references of my own, though these are kept to a minimum.

INTRODUCTION

1. V. I. Lénin, Party Organisation and Party Literature (see Appendix I).
2. Constitution of the Union of Writers as set out in *Pérvyi vsesoyúznyi s'yezd sovétskikh pisátelei: stenografícheskii otchët.*
3. In fact this is not quite true. What Shólokhov is recorded as saying is that he was 'not very good at scientific formulations'; but he went on to add: 'Socialist Realism is the art of the truth of life, comprehended and interpreted by the artist from the point of view of devotion to Leninist party principles.' *Socialist Realism in Literature and Art* (Moscow: Progress Publishers, 1971, trans. C. V. James) p. 85.

1 ART AND THE PEOPLE

The major source of the argument set out in this chapter was *Osnóvy mark. sístsko-léninskoi estétiki*, ed. A. Sutyágin *et al.* (Moscow: Gosizdát politícheskoi literátury, 1960), which may be regarded as representing an officially approved point of view.

1. See A. C. Wilson 'The Soviet Orthodoxy in Aesthetics, 1953–70', *New Zealand Slavonic Journal* (Winter, 1971, published by the Department of Russian of the Victoria University of Wellington).
2. *Osnóvy mark. sístsko-léninskoi estétiki* (Ak. Naúk S.S.S.R., 1960).
3. The word *naród* has an almost mystic ring to Russian ears, meaning far more than simply 'the people', and being closer, perhaps, to the German *Volk.* The root is extremely productive and care should be taken not to confuse *naródnichestvo* – which is usually translated 'populism' and *naród-*

nost'. The adjective *naródny* means 'pertaining to the people' and may thus be translated as 'popular', but when associated with *naródnost'* it has a more specific connotation, conveyed in this book by single inverted commas – thus 'popular'.

4. Certain Western commentators seem not to take this point. John Berger, for instance, takes 'popular' to mean 'universally liked' and then sets out to disprove his own erroneous interpretation (*Art and Revolution* (Penguin Books, 1969) p. 50).

5. Cf. Winston Churchill's alleged remark concerning the reconstruction of the House of Commons after bombing: '... We shape the buildings, then the buildings shape us.'

6. Collection *K. Marks i F. Engel's ob iskússtve* (Moscow: 'Iskússtvo', 1957) I 202.

7. Ibid., p. 152.

8. Hegel, *Sochinéniya,* XII 280.

9. Collection *K. Marks i F. Engel's ob iskússtve* I 250.

10. However, Marx's dictum that there would come a day when there were no professional artists but only men who, amongst other things, were artists, when reflected in Pletněv's article 'On the Ideological Front', *Právda,* 1922, as: 'The proletarian artist will be artist and worker at the same time' received very curt comment from Lénin in a pencilled margin note: 'Rubbish!' (*Vzdor*). Quoted by S. Sheshukóv, *Neístovye revníteli* (Moskóvskii rabóchii, 1970) p. 28.

11. Dobrolyúbov, *O stépeni uchástiya naródnosti v razvítiyi rússskoi literatúry.*

12. Nekrásov, *Komú na Rusí zhit' khoroshó? (For whom is life in Russia good?)*

13. Collection *V. I. Lénin o literatúre i iskússtve* (Goslitizdát, 1957) p. 583.

14. V. G. Belínsky, *Pólnoye sobrániye* (Ak. Naúk S.S.S.R., 1954) V 308.

15. Ibid., p. 309.

16. Collection *K. Marks i F. Engel's ob iskússtve,* p. 559.

17. Examples cited are the formation of the Moiséyev Folk-Dance Ensemble and the establishment of puppet theatres. Such reasoning explains the appearance in the USSR of 'modern traditional songs', i.e. songs in the folk idiom but concerned with such aspects of contemporary life as the factory, the collective farm and even space-travel. These should not be confused with artificially preserved – or invented – 'folksy' local colour.

18. Collection *V. I. Lénin o literatúre i iskússtve,* p. 254.

19. Collection *K. Marks i F. Engel's ob iskússtve,* I 112.

20. V. I. Lénin, *Kritícheskiye zamétki po natsionál 'nomu voprósu (Critical Notes on the Nationalities Question),* 1913; e.g. – 'In every national culture there are in fact two national cultures. There is the Great-Russian culture of the Purishkéviches, the Guchkóvs and the Strúves; but there is also the Great-Russian culture characterised by the names of Chernyshévsky and Plekhánov...'

21. Collection *K. Marks i F. Engel's ob iskússtve,* p. 134.

22. *Proletkult:* abbreviation for *Soyúz proletárskikh kul'túrnoprosvetítel'nikh organizátsii* (Union of Proletarian Cultural-Educative Organisations),

whose aim was to create a new, revolutionary proletarian art and to disregard the art of all previous epochs (see Chapter 3).

23. See Appendix III, *Documents on the Proletkult*.
24. Collection *K. Marks i F. Engel's ob iskússtve*, p. 99.
25. Ibid., pp. 116–17.
26. V. I. Lénin, *Pámyati Gértsena* trans. as *In Memory of Hérzen*, collection
    V. I. Lenin on Literature and Art (Moscow: Progress Publishers, 1970)
    pp. 63–9, given as Appendix II of this book.
27. V. I. Lénin, *L. N. Tolstói kak zérkalo rússkoi revolyútsiyi*, trans. as *L. N.
    Tolstoy as the Mirror of the Russian Revolution* in the collection *V. I.
    Lenin on Literature and Art*, pp. 28–33; see also pp. 48–62.
28. V. I. Lénin, *Partiinaya organizátsiya i partiinaya literatúra* (see Appendix I).
29. Collection *K. Marks i F. Engel's ob iskússtve*, 1 346–7.
30. See Karl Marx and Frederick Engels, *Selected Correspondence* (Moscow:
    Progress Publishers, 1965) pp. 73, 100, etc.; see also the article by Geórgi
    Kunítsyn, *Lenin on Partisanship and Freedom of Creativity* in the collec-
    tion *Socialist Realism in Literature and Art* (Moscow: Progress Publishers,
    1971).
31. Karl Marx and Frederick Engels, *Selected Correspondence*, pp. 116–20.
32. Ibid., pp. 401–3.
33. Ibid., pp. 390–1.
34. For a fuller discussion of *partiinost'* see the article by Geórgi Kunítsyn,
    note 30 (above).
35. See A. S. Myansikóv and Ya. Ye El'sbérg (eds), *Léninskoye naslédiye i
    literatúra XX véka* (Moscow: 'Khudózhestvennaya literatúra', 1969) p. 34.
36. *Vtorói vsesoyúznyi s'yezd sovétskikh pisátelei*, 1956 *(stenografícheskii
    otchët)*.

2 ART AND THE PARTY

The major source of the argument set out in the early sections of this chapter
was *V. I. Lénin i rússkaya obshchestvenno-politicheskaya mysl'XIX-nachala
XX v.*, ed. Sh. M. Lévin *et al.* Leningrad: Naúka, 1969).

1. V. I. Lénin, *Partiinaya (organizátsiya i partiinaya literatúra* (see Appendix
   I).
2. *Osnóvy marksístsko-léninskoi estétiki*, p. 337.
3. V. I. Lénin, *Partiinaya organizátsiya i partiinaya literatúra*.
4. See, for example, John Berger, *Revolution and Art* (Penguin Books, 1969)
   p. 54; see also Lukács, *Solzhenitsyn* (Merlin Press, 1970) p. 77.
5. V. I. Lénin, *Násha prográmma*, IV 182.
6. G. V. Plekhánov, *O sotsiál'noi demokrátiyi v Rossíyi*.
7. V. I. Lénin, *Násha blizháishaya zadácha*, IV 189–90.
8. V. I. Lénin, *Zádáchi rússkikh sotsiál-demokrátov*, II 459.
9. V. I. Lénin, *Násha prográmma*, IV, 184.
10. V. I. Lénin, *Iz próshlogo rabóchei pecháti v Rossíyi/From the History of the
    Workers' Press in Russia* (excerpts) in the collection *V. I. Lenin on Litera-
    ture and Art*, p. 97.
11. G. V. Plekhánov, speech in Geneva, *14 December 1825* made in 1900 and

quoted by Sh. M. Lévin *et al.* (eds), *V. I. Lénin i rússkaya obshchéestvenno-politícheskaya mysl' XIX-nachála XX v.* (Leningrad: Naúka, 1969) p. 17.

12. V. I. Lénin, *Chto délat'?/What is to be Done?*, trans. S. V. and P. Utéchin (Panther Books, 1970).

13. V. I. Lénin, *Pámyati Gértsena.*

14. Ibid.

15. N. V. Shelgunóv, *Délo* No. 3, 1881, quoted by Lévin *et al.*, *V. I. Lenin i rússkaya . . . obshchest.-pol. mysl'*, pp. 42–3.

16. V. I. Lénin, *Pámyati Gértsena.*

17. V. I. Lénin, *Ot kakógo naslédstva my otkázyvayemsya?*, II 530/*The Heritage we Renounce* in the collection *V. I. Lenin on Culture and Cultural Revolution* (Moscow: Progress Publishers, 1970).

18. V. I. Lénin, *Iz próshlogo rabóchei pecháti v Rossíyi.*

19. V. I. Lénin, *O Vékhakh, xix 169/Concerning Vekhi* in the collection *V. I. Lenin on Culture and Cultural Revolution.*

20. Cf. G. V. Plekhánov: 'Without a revolutionary theory there is no revolutionary movement in the true sense of the word'. *Selected Philosophical Works* (Moscow: Gospolitizdát, 1956), 195.

21. V. I. Lénin, *Chto délat'?*

22. V. I. Lénin, *Zadáchi rússkikh sotsiál-demokrátov.*

23. Sh. M. Lévin, S. N. Valk, V. S. Dyákin (eds), *V. I. Lénin i rússkaya obshchestvenno-politícheskaya mysl' XIX – nachála XX v.* (Leningrad: Naúka, 1969) pp. 35–40. Fascinating unexpected support for such a point of view is cited from Dostoyévsky, who, writing on the subject of the International, disagreed with the suggestion that Belínsky, had he lived longer, would have become a Slavophil: 'Belínsky . . . might have emigrated . . . and he would now be an enthusiastic little old man, his warm faith intact and admitting of no shadow of doubt, flitting from congress to congress in Germany and Switzerland.' F. M. Dostoyévsky, *Collected Works* (in Russian), v 152.

24. Ibid.

25. M. M. Essen, *Voprósy istóriyi*, 1955, No. 1. p. 28, quoted by Lévin *et al.*, *V. I. Lenin i russkaya . . . obshchest.-pol. mysl'.*

26. V. I. Lénin, *Chto takóye 'Druz'yá naróda' . . ./What are 'The Friends of the People . . .',* in the collection *V. I. Lenin on Literature and Art.*

27. Ibid.

28. See N. K. Krúpskaya, *O Lénine. Sbórnik stat'yéi i vystuplénii* (Moscow: Izdátel'stvo politícheskoi literatúry, 1971) 281–2.

29. V. I. Lenin, *Krestyánskaya refórma*, p. 175.

30. *K. Marks, F. Engel's i revolyutsiónnaya Rossíya* (Moscow, 1967) pp. 48, 226.

31. Lenin's article *Ot kakógo naslédstva . . .* was intended for the journal *Nóvoye slóvo (New Word)*, but this was closed down so it subsequently appeared under a pseudonym (Vladímir Ilyín) in a collection of articles. Even so, Lénin could not refer directly to Chernyshévsky and directed his attention ostensibly to a book by Skáldin, whom he described as 'in general extraordinarily mediocre'.

32. In the journal *Rússkoye bogátstvo*, October 1897.

33. 'He loved Chernyshévsky's novel *What is to be Done?*, despite its artistic

ally inferior and naïve form. I was surprised how attentively he read this novel...' N. K. Krúpskaya, *O. Lénine* ... , p. 75.

34. Cf. Mao Tse-tung's development of this theme: 'Life as reflected in works of literature and art can and ought to be on a higher plane, more intense, more concentrated, more typical, nearer the ideal, and therefore more universal than actual everyday life.' *Talks at the Yenan Forum on Literature and Art, May 1942* (Peking: Foreign Languages Press, 1967).

35. A. V. Lunachársky, *Stat'yí o literatúre* (Moscow, 1957) p. 118.

36. V. I. Lénin, *Proyékt réchi po agrárnomu voprósu vo vtorói Gosudárstvennoi dúme*, xv 152–3.

37. K. Marks, F. Engel's i revolyutsiónnaya Rossíya.

38. V. I. Lénin, *Ot kakógo naslédstva* ...

39. *V. I. Lénin o literatúre i iskusstve* (Moscow, 1967) p. 665.

40. Contrast D. S. Mírsky's assessment of Dobrolyúbov's work: 'Although all his criticism is about works of imaginative literature, it would be grossly unjust to call it literary criticism.' *A History of Russian Literature* (Routledge & Kegan Paul, 1949) p. 215.

41. *K. Marks, F. Engel's i revolyutsiónnaya Rossíya.*

42. N. A. Dobrolyúbov, quoted in Zerchanínov, Ráikhin, Strázhev, *Rússkaya literatúra* (Moscow: Uchpedgiz, 1948) pp. 132–5.

43. D. I. Písarev, *Prómakhi nezréloi mýsli*, in *Rússkoye slóvo* in 1864; see D. I. Písarev, *Collected Works* (in Russian), (Moscow, 1956) III 147–9.

44. V. I. Lénin, *Chto délat'?* pp. 171–3.

45. *V. I. Lénin o literatúre i iskússtve*, p. 250.

46. See N. K. Krúpskaya, *O Lénine* ... pp. 75, 239, etc.; also quoted by Zerchanínov *et al.*, op. cit.

47. V. I. Lénin, *Anarkhízm i sotsialízm*, v 377–8.

48. V. I. Lénin, *Gosudárstvo i revolyútsiya*, xxxiii 103–4.

49. P. N. Tkachëv, *Selected Works* (in Russian), III (Moscow, 1933) quoted by Lévin *et al.*, op. cit.

50. *Istóriya Vsesoyúznoi Kommunistícheskoi Pártiyi (Bol'shevikóv)*, (Moscow: Gosizdat. polit. lit., 1938) p. 12.

51. From the verb *peredvigat'sya* – 'to shift, travel, move about'; when the original 'Workshop of Free Artists' broke up, a number of its members formed a 'Brotherhood of Travelling Exhibitions' to take an annual exhibition 'to the people'. The name 'Wanderers' is sometimes used, though with its connotations of aimlessness, it is hardly precise.

52. See *Istóriya rússkogo iskússtva (Akadémiya khudózhestv S.S.S.R.*, (Moscow Gosizdat. 'Iskússtvo', 1960) vol. II. See also Zerchanínov *et al.*, op. cit.

53. Quoted by Zerchanínov *et al.*, p. 146.

54. Ibid., p. 153.

55. K. N. Leónt'yev, *Vostók, Rossíya i slavyánstvo* (Moscow, 1883) II 86, quoted by Lévin *et al.*

56. *Istóriya Vsesoyúznoi Kommunistícheskoi Pártiyi (Bol'shevikóv)*, p. 12.

57. V. I. Lénin, *Zadáchi rússkikh sotsiál-demokrátov*, II 464.

58. G. V. Plekhánov, *Collected Works* (in Russian), (Moscow–Petrograd, 1924) II 255, quoted by Lévin *et al.*

59. Quoted in *Istóriya rússkoi literatúry*, IX 84.

60. V. I. Lénin, *Pobéda kadétov i zadáchi rabóchei pártiyi*, XII 331.
61. See K. Marx and F. Engels, *Selected Correspondence*, pp. 383–4, etc.
62. But see Lenin's comments on Strúve in *Kritícheskiye zamétki po natsionál' nomu voprósu*.
63. In *Náshi raznoglásiya* Plekhánov had also advocated the formation of a party: 'The earliest possible organisation of a workers' party is the only means of resolving all the economic and political contradictions of present-day Russia.' *Selected Philosophical Works* (Moscow: Gospolitizdát, 1956) I 364.

3 A Few Decrees...

1. O Proletkúl'takh. Pis'mó TsK, R.K.P. (*Pravda*, No. 270, 1 December 1920). See Appendix III of this volume.
2. The name of Trótsky receives increasing mention in contemporary Soviet writing, but always in a 'negative' context, e.g.: 'In this, as in everything, he distorted and subverted Lénin's teaching. In his book, *Literature and Revolution*, he argued at great length that in the period of transition from capitalism to socialism – the period of its dictatorship – the ruling class would be in a state of constant struggle with the enemy and would have no time for building a new culture. Throughout this period the workers would assimilate the old bourgeois-aristocratic culture and literature, and only in the distant future, when they had assimilated the old, would they begin to build a new socialist culture and literature.' S. Sheshukóv, *Neístovyye revníteli* (Moskóvskii rabóchii, 1970) p. 31.
3. Leon Trótsky, *Literature and Revolution* (Ann Arbor Paperbacks, University of Michigan Press, 1960).
4. *Vystupléniye na díspute 'Pérvyye kámni nóvoi kul'túry'*, in the collection *Nóvoye o Mayakóvskom* (Moscow: Ak. Naúk U.S.S.R., 1958).
5. Lunachársky's Commissariat was responsible for pre-school education, schools and higher educational establishments, professional training and the liquidation of illiteracy; science, museums and ancient monuments; literature and the theatre; cultural–educative work and publishing. Such a list is indicative of the relationship seen to exist between the items in it.
6. V. V. Mayakóvsky, *Ya sam*, 1922–28.
7. Belief in the ability to create works of art without the need for any kind of training was a feature of the Proletkult credo.
8. *O Proletkúl'takh*.
9. The title given to a volume of art reproductions published to commemorate the Fiftieth Anniversary of the Revolution.
10. A term used by Zhdánov but attributed by him to Stálin.
11. Lénin was not himself over-enthusiastic: 'Spectacles are not really great art. I would sooner call them more or less attractive entertainment.' *Socialist Realism in Literature and Art*, p. 28.
12. Quoted by G. Trélin, *Léninskii lózung 'Iskússtvo – naródu!' i stanovléniye sovétskoi muzykál'noi kul'túry* (Moscow: Izd. 'Múzyka', 1970).
13. *V. I. Lénin o literatúre i iskússtve*, p. 665.
14. See, for example, the Futurist Manifesto – *Poshchëchina obshchéstvennomu vkúsu* (*A Slap in the Face of Public Taste*), 1912, a full translation of

which may be found in V. Markov, *Russian Futurism* (MacGibbon & Kee, 1969) pp. 45–6.

15. *V. I. Lénin o literatúre i iskússtve.*

16. One of the first writers to respond to the new government's invitation to individuals to co-operate with it.

17. Quoted by Sheila Fitzpatrick, *The Commissariat of Enlightenment* (Cambridge University Press, 1971).

18. Lenin's policy toward non-Russians is illustrated by the role allotted to national languages in this decree: 'All the population of the Republic between the ages of 8 and 50 who are unable to read and write are required to take up study either in their native language, or in Russian, according to choice.' Rather than attempting to suppress the national languages – 'the kernel of national consciousness' – he wished to enlist them as media for the propagation of Marxism. See V. I. Lenin, *Questions of National Policy and Proletarian Internationalism* (Moscow: Foreign Languages Publishing House, 1960).

19. Púnin, *In the Days of Red October*, quoted by Sheila Fitzpatrick.

20. For a very detailed account of the period see E. H. Carr, *A History of Soviet Russia*, 9 vols. (Macmillan, 1950–69) also available in a Penguin Books edition.

21. See, for example, *Istóriya Kommunistícheskoi Pártiyi Sovétskogo Soyúza* (Moscow: Gospolitizdát, 1960).

22. Ibid.

23. The term 'artistic literature' (*khudózhestvennaya literatúra*) is used to distinguish this from writing in general.

24. The word *pechát'* is ambiguous and may refer either to printed matter in general or to the 'press' in the sense of newspapers and journals in particular. For the latter, the borrowed word *préssa* may also now be found.

25. The Party had made its position clear at the IXth Congress in April, which had resolved: 'To acknowledge the necessity for educational work in the field of the arts, both to preserve the best models of the old art in all its forms and take measures to acquaint the masses with them on a broad basis, and to sponsor and facilitate the development of proletarian and peasant forms of culture and the emergence of revolutionary art.'

26. Quoted by G. Trélin, *Léninskii lózung . . .*

27. Lunachársky underlined Lénin's capacity for 'revolutionary–romantic' vision combined with practical realism, recalling how Lénin had reprimanded him for objecting to the possible damage to historic buildings during the struggle with the Provisional Government in 1917: 'How can you possibly attach such importance to some old building, however fine, when we are concerned with opening the doors to a social system able to create beauty immeasurably greater than could even have been dreamed of in the past?' See I. M. Térekhov (ed.), *A. V. Lunachársky. Statyí o sovétskoi literatúre* (Moscow: 'Prosveshchéniye', 1971).

28. Pletnëv's article 'On the Ideological Front', *Pravda* (September 1922) had reopened the argument, and Yákovlev's reply 'On Proletarian Culture and the Proletkult' in the same paper soon after was constructed on the basis of Lénin's comments and may therefore be said to represent his views. In

his own letter to the paper, Lénin said: 'But this is *falsification* of historical materialism. It is playing at historical materialism.' (quoted by I. M. Térekhov).

29. V. I. Lénin, *Draft Resolution 'On Proletarian Culture'*, see Appendix III.

30. Krúpskaya related how Lénin refused to join the god-seeking activities of Bogdánov and Górky on Capri in 1905: 'I cannot and will not have anything to do with people who have set out to propagate unity between scientific socialism and religion.' In fact he did go to Capri but no reconciliation resulted. N. K. Krúpskaya, *Memories of Lenin* (Panther Books, 1970).

31. *V. I. Lénin o literatúre i iskússtve*, p. 684.

32. Lunachársky was Bogdánov's brother-in-law and had also been involved in the god-seeking controversy.

33. At a later date Lunachársky himself acknowledged the justice of Lénin's fears: 'Lénin talked about this when it had not even entered my head, and I simply could not see it...' *Rússkaya literatúra pósle Oktyabryá*, a lecture delivered at Sverdlóvsk University in February 1929 (quoted by I. M. Térekhov).

34. By 1920 the Proletkults had some 400,000 members, of whom as many as 80,000 were actively working in clubs, studios, theatres, etc.

35. The Futurist Manifesto, proclaimed over the names of Burlyúk, Kruchënykh, Mayakóvsky and Khlébnikov in 1912, had said: 'Throw Púshkin, Dostoyévsky, Tolstóy *et al., et al.*, overboard from the Ship of Modernity...' (for full text, see V. Markov, *Russian Futurism*).

36. *Nóvoye o Mayakóvskom* (See Chapter 4, note 4).

37. *V. I. Lénin on Literature and Art*, p. 214. For original, see *Nóvoye o Mayakóvskom*.

38. According to Lunachársky's first wife, this protest was in fact prompted by Lénin (quoted by I. M. Térekhov, p. 524).

39. A. V. Lunachársky, *Lózhka protivoyádiya* in the journal *Iskússtvo Kommúny*, 1918 (quoted by I. M. Térekhov).

40. *V. I. Lénin o literatúre i iskússtve*, pp. 662–3.

41. A. V. Lunachársky, letter to A. K. Vorónsky, 1923, quoted by I. M. Térekhov.

42. For a discussion of NEP see Alec Nove, *An Economic History of the U.S.S.R.* (Pelican Books. 1972).

43. Although the task of educating the peasantry has dominated much of Soviet policy ever since the Revolution, the Proletkult had tended to ignore it, and this was another reason for Lénin's antipathy.

44. The 'Old Guard' was a name coined by Lénin (in a letter to Mólotov in March 1922: XXXIII 228–30) to refer to the veteran Bolsheviks of pre-revolutionary vintage. It highlighted a basic dilemma: the 'Old Guard', all occupying positions of great authority, had lost their class identity, but the new influx of party members undoubtedly contained many who were petty bourgeois in outlook and therefore unreliable. So in the period of the 'dictatorship of the proletariat', that proletariat hardly existed and, where it did, had very little authority.

45. ROSTA – the Russian Telegraph Agency, whose posters, drawn in many

cases by Mayakóvsky, were displayed in windows, first in Moscow and then in other towns during the Civil War, showing the progress at the fronts and propagandising such matters as medical inoculations, liquidation of illiteracy, etc. and antireligion. Such posters may still be seen in large cities.

46. For a discussion of the state of the Soviet cinema see George A. Huaco, *The Sociology of Film Art* (New York–London: Basic Books, Inc., 1965). See also Jay Leyda, *Kino* (Allen and Unwin, 1960); and V. Zhdan (ed.), *Krátkaya istóriya sovétskogo kinó, 1917–67* ('Iskússtvo', 1969).

47. The numerous groups whose abbreviated titles end in APP were all Associations of Proletarian Writers (*proletpisátelei*): hence RAPP (*Rossíiskaya* – Russian); VAPP (*Vserossíiskaya* – All-Russian); MAPP (*Moskóvskaya* – Moscow); VOAPP (*Vsesoyúznoye ob'yedineniye…* – All-Union League), etc.

48. One factor complicating Soviet policy was that in national areas the industrial proletariat tended to consist of Russians, and the peasantry – of indigenous inhabitants. The usual worker/peasant rift therefore took on a national or even racial aspect. Moreover the number of literate nationals who were not actively anti-Soviet bourgeois was so small that local organs of government were almost always in the hands of Russians or Ukrainians. Hence the urgency of the education programme for nationals, coupled with a degree of centralisation sufficient to prevent the emergence of 'bourgeois nationalism'. See Geoffrey Wheeler, *Racial Problems in Soviet Muslim Asia* (Oxford University Press, 1960).

49. 'Fellow-traveller' (*popútchik*) was a name coined by Trótsky to refer to non-Marxist intellectuals, especially writers, who supported the Party without belonging to it. He described them as 'manure for proletarian culture' and said 'They will not come with us to the very end'. In fact, the term became used of anyone not actually associated with RAPP and was thus something of a misnomer when applied to many contemporary writers.

50. The 1922 Party Congress passed a resolution 'On Anti-Soviet Parties and Movements' which stated that legal publishers had become 'means of agitation against the regime of the peasants and workers'.

51. The journal *Chronicle of the House of Littérateurs* (*Létopis' dóma literátorov*) is quoted by Sheshukóv (Néistovyye revníteli, Moskóvskii rabóchii, 1970) as stating: '… it is time to realise that peace with the intelligentsia is even more important than peace with the bourgeoisie. The government cannot live without its brain, the intelligentsia.' (No. 3, 1921, p. 11.)

52. Cf. Chapter 3, note 28.

53. By this time the MAPP *Oktyábr'* group had gained effective control of VAPP, though *Kúznitsa* disputed its right to it.

54. Education, in such contexts, should be understood to refer not to the opening up of possibilities for freedom of choice and individual decision but to *information* (the passing on of data) and *indoctrination* (persuasion or coercion to accept a certain point of view). Something of this distinction is conveyed in the Russian anecdote which defines an optimist as an indoctrinated pessimist and a pessimist as an informed optimist!

55. Cf. Fadéyev: 'We should write simply, but in a juicy and lively manner. We should write in a language intelligible to the working masses.'

56. Cf. Constitution of the Union of Writers, given in: *Pervyi vsesoyúznyi s'yezd sovétskikh pisátelei*: *stenografícheskii otchët*, 1934).

57. It is significant that a very high proportion of prominent Soviet writers began their careers by contributing to newspapers.

58. See Moshe Lewin, *Lenin's Last Struggle* (Faber & Faber, 1969; translated from French).

59. See, for example, R. M. Hankin, 'Soviet Literary Controls', in *Continuity and Change in Russian and Soviet Thought*, ed. E. J. Simmons (Harvard University Press, 1955).

60. *Nóvoye o Mayakóvskom*.

61. *Kapitulyánstvo*: an invented pejorative label formed on the root *kapitulyátsiya* (capitulation) and applied to attitudes considered to operate to the advantage of capitalism at the expense of socialism.

62. Initial members were VAPP, the All-Russian Union of Peasant Writers, and the Constructivists' Literary Centre, and these were later joined by *Kúznitsa* and *Perevál* – the fellow-travellers' organisation formed as a defence against RAPP. The Constructivists later withdrew. A significant feature was the use of the title *Soviet*, which made it possible to avoid stressing the proletarian or bourgeois composition.

63. *Komsomól* – Communist Youth League, an organisation including members up to their mid-twenties formed to assist the C.P.S.U. and acting, in part, as a recruiting and training agency.

64. Western visitors to the USSR are frequently surprised at the political nature of Soviet youth organisations. In fact they have little in common with such organisations as the Scouts.

65. The 1921 Party Congress had accepted a ban on inner-party factions.

66. For an exciting account of the Trótsky/Stálin confrontations see Isaac Deutscher, *The Prophet Unarmed* (Oxford Paperbacks, 1970).

67. As editor of *Pravda*, Bukhárin was a powerful ally of Stálin at this time.

68. *Na literatúrnom postú* (which replaced *Na postú* after 1925), No. 9, 1927, p. 2, quoted by Sheshukóv.

69. See, for example, V. Shcherbína's argument in the article 'O nékotorykh voprósakh sotsialistícheskogo realízma' in the collection *Za vysókuyu idéinost' sovetskoi literatúry* (Moscow: Gos khudlit, 1959).

70. *Na literatúrnom postú*, No. 9, 1927, p. 2 (quoted by Sheshukóv).

71. A prime mover in the RAPP enthusiasm for Tolstoyan methods of characterisation had been Fadéyev.

72. See our discussion of Písarev (Chapter 2).

73. Cf. Stálin's speech to the *Komsomól* Congress in May, 1928: 'We cannot now confine ourselves to training Communist forces *in general*, Bolshevik forces *in general*, people who are able to jabber a little about anything. Dilettanteism and universalism are now fetters on our ankles. What we now need are Bolshevik *specialists* ...': Joseph Stálin, *The Tasks of Youth* (New York: International Publishers) p. 28 (undated).

74. For a detailed account of this controversy see Sheshukóv, pp. 216–26.

75. Yermílov: a resilient critic-cum-literary bureaucrat whose attacks on Mayakóvsky influenced the poet's mood at the time of his suicide and who was mentioned in the suicide note (see *Nóvoye o Mayakóvskom*).

76. Quoted by Sheshukóv.

77. *Pilnyakóvshchina*: the point of view ascribed to Borís Pilnyák, who saw the Revolution as a movement of the whole people and denied the leading role of the proletariat and Russian Communist Party (R.C.P.). In *Fragments From a Diary* he wrote: 'I am not a Communist... and I do not admit that I should write like a Communist.... Communist power in Russia is determined by Russia's historic fate, not by the will of the Communists. ... In so far as the Communists are with Russia, I am with them.... The fate of the R.C.P. interests me much less than the fate of Russia. For me, the R.C.P. is just another link in the chain of Russian history...'

78. Of special interest to the student of the period is the composition of the editorial board: Górky, Kaganóvich, Póstyshev, Andréyev, Yenukídze, Stétsky, Bukhárin, Pyatakóv, Shvérnik, Kósarev, Tsíkhon, Bogushévsky, Vs. Ivánov, Averbákh, Grónsky, Gástev, Pankrátova, Mékhlis, N. Popóv, Zhíga, Libedínsky, Kolotílov, Térekhov, Samóilov, Chumándrin, Záitsev, A. Písarev, Krívov, Tsiperóvich, Seifúllina.

79. In particular in its opposition to the Perevérzev group and the fellow-travellers' organisation, *Perevál*, which had been weakened by the removal of Vorónsky.

80. The terms *rost... úrovnya* (growth of level) and *povysháyet... rol'* (raises ... the role) are typical of the infelicitous uses of language that begin to appear in party statements in the late twenties.

81. OGIZ: *Ob'yedinéniye gosudárstvennykh izdátel'stv* – Union of State Publishers, formed in 1930 and discontinued since 1949.

82. Pioneers: the junior youth movement, based largely on the school.

83. In fact children's literature did attract a number of very important writers in the thirties, of whom perhaps Yúrii Olésha, Nikolái Zabolótskii and Yevgénii Shvarts are especially worthy of mention. The assertion by some commentators that children's literature was 'safer' for writers of dubious ideological purity seems unlikely, in the context of the Party's attitude expressed in this statement, to have been entirely true, though it might have seemed so for a while.

84. From a draft *On the basis of policy in the field of the arts*, prepared by the Arts Sector of *Narkomprós* and *Rabís* (Workers' Inspectorate), quoted from *Sovétskoye iskússtvo za 15 let* (Moscow–Leningrad, 1933) by G. Trélin.

85. Cf. Zhdánov's speech at the First Writers' Congress in 1934: '... the fundamental difficulties have already been overcome.... Our country has finished laying the foundations of a socialist economy.... The socialist way of life has incontrovertibly and finally triumphed.' A. A. Zhdánov, *On Literature, Music and Philosophy* (Lawrence & Wishart, 1950).

86. An expression used by Izaák Bábel' at the first Writers' Congress.

87. Nikolái Ostróvsky's *Kak zakalyálas' stal'* (*How the Steel was Tempered*), written during the period 1930–4, is considered a classic of socialist-realist fiction of the thirties. It is perhaps worth noting that 'Stalin' means 'man of steel'.

88. *Pérvyi vsesoyúznyi s'yezd sovétskikh pisátelei* (*stenografícheskii otchët*).

89. In 1931 the RAPP leadership had quarrelled both with the *Komsomól* and with the Central Committee, C.P.S.U.

90. The term *popútchik* – 'fellow-traveller' was never officially adopted; there is, however, an officially recognised category of *bezpartiinyi* – 'one without a party', i.e. one who supports the policies of the CPSU but is not himself a member.

91. A part cause of the venom with which Sinyávsky was attacked was the fact that inside the USSR he enjoyed a considerable reputation as an 'establishment' critic. The key article on Górky in the 1958 Academy of Sciences three-volume *History of Russian Soviet Literature*, for example, bears his signature.

92. For details of the operation of *Glavlít* see *The Politics of Ideas in the U.S.S.R.*, ed. Robert Conquest (Bodley Head, 1967).

93. See, for example, Sheshukóv.

4 SOCIALIST REALISM

1. *Osnóvy marksístsko-léninskoi estétiki.*

2. Ibid., quoted from *O polítike pártiyi v óblasti literatúry i iskússtva* (Ak. obshchéstvennykh naúk, Central Committee, CPSU, 1958) p. 111.

3. See Pável Kórin, 'Thoughts on Art' in the collection *Socialist Realism in Literature and Art.*

4. 'Pérvaya vstrécha s Mayakóvskym v 1917', in the collection *Nóvoye o Mayakóvskom* (Moscow: Ak: Naúk S.S.S.R., 1958) p. 571, quoting a letter from Lunachárky to his wife on 1 July 1917. In this letter the Commíssar praises Mayakóvsky's talent, but in the following year in the final (unpublished) section of an article for *Iskússtvo kommúny* (*The Art of the Commune*) he says: 'But Vladímir Mayakóvsky worries me greatly.... He promises well in maturity, but his maturity is too long delayed...' And in 1925, at the debate *Pérvyye kámni nóvoi kul'túry* (see Chapter 3) he returns to this assessment, saying that Mayakóvsky will *always* be immature.

　　The collection *Nóvoye o Mayakóvskom*, edited by Academician V. V. Vinográdov *et al.*, was intended to be the first of two volumes. However, the second volume never appeared and the first was withdrawn a year after publication because it presented material that showed Mayakóvsky in an unfavourable light. The Central Committee statement on 31 March 1959 reproved the editors and said: 'The reactionary press in other countries is using the book ... for anti-Soviet purposes.'

5. See Gleb Strúve, *Soviet Russian Literature* (University of Oklahoma Press, 1951).

6. In *The New Men*, for example, C. P. Snow has one of his characters claim that people 'not far removed from the party line' betray their allegiance by referring to things as 'Soviet' rather than 'Russian'!

7. Various works have been reappraised at different periods and consequently revised; e.g. Fadéyev, *Molodáya Gvárdiya* (*The Young Guard*) etc.

8. Constitution of the Union of Writers: in *Pérvyi vsesoyúznyi s'yezd sovétskikh pisátelei* (*Stenografícheskii otchét*).

9. N. S. Khrushchëv in the collection *Za tésnuyu svyaz' literatúry i iskússtva s zhízn'yu naróda* (Iskússtvo, 1958) pp. 64–5.

10. Contrast the 'formalist' attitude as expressed by L. L. Sabanéyev in the

Journal of the Association for Contemporary Music in the early 1920s: 'Music does not and cannot include any ideology within itself.... It is a self-contained world, from which any break into logic and ideology can be accomplished only by violent and artificial means.' *Muzykál'naya kul'túra*, No. 1, p. 11, 1924, quoted by G. Trélin.

11. *Právda*, 27 November 1955.

12. Directed by Tráuberg and Kózintsev: *The Youth of Maksím* (1935), *The Return of Maksím* (1937), and *The Výborg Side* (1939).

13. An outstanding example of concern with a topical issue was with the campaign for peace during the Khrushchëv era.

14. Examples of unsuccessful films from this point of view are cited as: *Belínsky*, dir. Kózintsev, 1951, and *Rímsky-Kórsakov*, dir. Roshál' and Kazénsky, 1952.

15. In polemics with Mayakóvsky, Lunachársky referred to formalism as 'spitting on life' (*naplevísm na zhizn'*); see *Nóvoye o Mayakóvskom*.

16. See our discussion of Písarev in Chapter 2.

17. Cf. M. A. Súslov's speech commemorating the 53rd Anniversary of the October Revolution on 6 November 1970: 'Armed with the theory of Marxism–Leninism, the Communist Party... embodies the ability to foresee the course of social development, to chart a correct political course of action and... to adhere to this course...' *Forward to the triumph of Communism under the banner of the Great October Revolution* (Moscow: Nóvosti Press, 1970).

18. *The Vow*, dir. Gelováni, 1942; *The Cranes are Flying*, dir. Kalatózov, 1957; *The Communist*, dir. Ráizmann, 1958; *A Man's Fate*, dir. Bondarchúk, 1959; *Ballad of a Soldier*, dir. Chukhrái, 1959. Note the Chinese estimate of this last film: '... In keeping with the purpose and task of the Soviet revisionist clique to spread the dread of war and peddle the philosophy of survival...' *Soviet Film in the Service of All-Round Capitalist Restoration* (Peking: Renmin Ribao, 30 October 1967).

19. *The Baltic Deputy*, dir. Zárkhi and Khéifits, 1936; *The Great Citizen*, dir. Ermler, 1937–9.

20. *Trétii s'yezd pisátelei S.S.S.R. (Stenografícheskii otchët)*, (Sovétskii pisátel', 1959) p. 249.

21. Examples cited are Dovzhénko's film, *Poem of the Sea* (*Poéma o móre*) 1958, and Mayakóvsky's poetry.

22. To a great extent this is still true and accounts in part for the apparent conservatism of Soviet literature and art. The Western appreciation of things Soviet is often a little out of focus because viewed from the point of view of life in the big cities, which should not be taken as typical.

23. *V. I. Lénin o literatúre i iskússtve*, p. 395.

24. Lénin agreed that the book showed signs of having been written in haste but greeted it as 'a very timely book' (*svoyevrémennaya kníga*). See *Socialist Realism in Literature and Art*.

25. *Vneocherednói XXI s'yezd Kommunistícheskoi Pártiyi Sovétskogo Soyúza. Stenografícheskii otchët*, 61–2.

26. Ibid.

27. A. Kosýgin's speech concerning the ninth five-year plan: 'Of great im-

portance for the fuller satisfaction of the people's cultural requirements is a
further expansion of book publishing, of the circulation of newspapers and
magazines, raising their ideological level and improving their design, developing the network of theatres, cinemas and film-projecting installations,
and providing more facilities for cultural institutions.' *Directives of the
Five-Year Economic Development Plan of the U.S.S.R. for 1971–75* (Moscow: Nóvosti Press, 1971).

28. Western visitors to the USSR are frequently horrified at being drawn
into amateur concerts (*samodéyatel'nost'*) and expected to perform themselves. The tendency to attribute the Soviet passion for this *samodéyatel'-
nost'* to the absence of more sophisticated means of entertainment and
the consequent necessity to 'make one's own fun' is, however, not entirely
justified.

29. Górky's term for literature in this sense was *chelovèkovédeniye* – 'the
study of man'.

30. Perhaps the most graphic evidence of this was the theatre, which played
to half-empty houses (almost inconceivable in Russia) for much of the
Stálin period. See A. Kron, *Zamétki pisátelya* (Moscow: Literatúrnaya
Moskvá, 1956), which incurred official odium, though the message was
clearly received. But see also Clause 45 of the party 'Resolution on the Questions of Propaganda, the Press and Agitation', 1923, which we discuss in
Chapter 3, on the use of the theatre as a vehicle for propaganda.

31. At its worst, *cosmopolitanism* is used, like *Zionísm*, as a term of abuse and
incitement to anti-semitism. See the Central Committee's decision 'on the
Journals '*Zvezdá*' and '*Leningrád*' ', 14 August 1946.

32. *Vtorói Vsesoyúznyi s'yezd sovétskikh pisátelei. Stenografícheskii otchët,*
p. 7.

33. L. Brézhnev, *Report of the Central Committee of the Communist Party of
the Soviet Union* (Moscow: Nóvosti Press Agency Publishing House,
1971).

34. Contrast Lukács' argument that the Stálin era *must* be explored in literature, since it is the past from which the present stems, and without a
knowledge of it the present can never be fully comprehended: 'The central problem of socialist realism today is to come to terms critically with
the Stálin era.' Georg Lukács, *Solzhenitsyn* (Merlin Press, 1969) p. 10.

35. Cf. Yákovlev (*Pravda*): '. . . and as regards art that has the temerity to call
itself proletarian, we have the right to make rather greater demands on it
than we might of the Maly Theatre.'

36. K. P. Thompson, 'Through the Smoke of Budapest', *The Reasoner*, No. 3
(November 1956) Supplement 6; quoted by Neal Wood, *Communism and
British Intellectuals* (Gollancz, 1959).

37. V. I. Lénin, *Draft Resolution 'On Proletarian Culture'*. See Appendix III.

38. But see Moshe Lewin, *Lenin's Last Struggle* (Faber & Faber, 1969; translated from the French).

39. *On the Party's Policy in the Field of Literature* (see Chapter 3 and Appendix IV).

40. *On the Reformation of Literary-Artistic Organisations* (see Appendix V).

41. V. I. Lénin: *Party Organisation and Party Literature* (see Appendix I).

APPENDIX I LÉNIN: PARTY ORGANISATION AND PARTY LITERATURE

1. This translation is taken from *Lenin on Literature and Art* (Moscow: Progress Publishers, 1970).
2. The political strike of October 1905, which compelled the Tsar to issue the Manifesto of 17 October, granting civil rights. The Bolsheviks took advantage of this new freedom to bring out their newspapers legally. After the failure of the armed rising in December 1905, the workers' organisations and press were again attacked.
3. *Bulletin of the Soviet Workers' Deputies*: the organ of the St Petersburg Soviet of Workers' Deputies, published from October to December 1905. Ten issues were published; the eleventh was seized by the police.
4 A. I. Guchkóv (1862–1936), industrialist and leader of the bourgeois-landowner Octobrist Party; he emigrated after the Bolshevik Revolution of 1917.
5. *Proletáry*: an illegal newspaper founded by the Bolsheviks after the Fourth Congress of the RSDLP, published 1906–9 in Finland and later in Geneva. Closed down in 1910 by decision of the Central Committee. Permanent editor, Lénin.

APPENDIX II LÉNIN: IN MEMORY OF HÉRZEN

1. This translation is taken from *Lenin on Literature and Art* (Moscow: Progress Publishers, 1970).
2. *Biron, E. J.* (1690–1772): a favourite of the Russian Empress Anna Ioannovna who acquired great influence over her policies and gained a reputation for terror.
3. *Arakchéyev, A. A.* (1769–1884): a favourite of the Tsars Paul I and Alexander I, responsible for a repressive, police regime.
4. *Manílov*: a character in Gogol's novel *Dead Souls*; regarded as a symbol of sentimental philistinism.
5. The Decembrists, who revolted against the Tsar in 1825.
6. A. I. Hérzen, *Ends and Beginnings*.
7. A. I. Hérzen, *To an Old Comrade*, letters 4 and 2.
8. *Narodism*, usually translated in Western works as *Populism*.
9. *Social-Revolutionaries*: a petty-bourgeois party which arose in 1901–2 as a result of a union of various populist groups. In 1917 it formed the mainstay of the Provisional Government.
10. *Trudoviks*: the group of petty-bourgeois democrats in the State Dumas, formed in 1906 and comprising peasants and intellectuals with populist leanings.
11. *Peasant Union*: the All-Russian Peasant Union—a revolutionary democratic organisation formed in 1905 with a radical but half-hearted programme of reform. Ceased to exist in 1907.
12. *Kólokol (The Bell)*: a revolutionary political journal published by Hérzen and Ogaryëv in London (1857–65) and Geneva (1865–8).

13. *Polyárnaya Zvezdá (The Pole Star)*: a literary political series of 8 volumes published by Hérzen alone (vols. I–III) and with Ogaryëv in London, 1855–62 and Geneva, 1868.

14. *Serno-Solovyévich, A. A.* (1838–69): prominent revolutionary democrat of the 1860s who emigrated in 1862 and criticised Hérzen for his liberal waverings.

15. *Kavélin, K. D.* (1818–85): professor of history at Moscow and St Petersburg, represented bourgeois landlord-liberalism and opposed the revolutionary-democrat movement.

16. The article was written by Ogaryëv.

17. *Cadet*: from the initials K. D. – Constitutional Democrat – the main party of the liberal-monarchist bourgeoisie, founded in 1905 and the prime opponent of the Soviet regime in the Civil War.

18. A. I. Hérzen, *N. G. Chernyshévsky*.

19. A. I. Hérzen, *Gossip, Soot, Grime, etc.*

20. A. I. Hérzen in a letter to Turgénev, 10 April 1864.

21. A. I. Hérzen, *Primordial Bishop, Antediluvian Government and Deceived People*.

22. *Naródnaya Vólya (People's Will)*: secret political organisation of populist terrorists formed in 1879 by a split in the major populist *Zemlyá i Vólya* (Land and Will). It was responsible for the assassination of Tsar Alexander II in 1881 and was stamped out in the consequent reprisals.

APPENDIX III (1) LÉNIN ON PROLETARIAN CULTURE;
(2) ON THE PROLETCULTS

1. The translation of this section is taken from *Lenin on Art and Literature* (Moscow: Progress Publishers, 1970).

2. My own translation – C.V.J.

3. Official Soviet translations use the word *education* for the Russian *prosveshchéniye*, which may otherwise denote enlightenment. Despite the enormously wide-ranging brief of the first People's Commissariat of Education, the use of the word *prosveshchéniye* was simply inherited from previous epochs.

4. October 1917.

5. Machism – empirio-criticism, a subjective-idealist philosophical trend initiated by the Austrian physicist and philosopher Ernst Mach, at the turn of the century and widespread in Western Europe. Amongst Bolshevik leaders associated at some period with this 'deviationist' line were Bogdánov, Bazárov and Lunachársky.

6. *God-building*: an attempt to reconcile scientific socialism and religion by a section of the intelligentsia disillusioned by the outcome of the 1905 revolution. Prominent in this movement were Bogdánov, Bazárov, Lunachársky and Górky.

APPENDIX IV   PARTY POLICY IN THE FIELD OF LITERATURE

1. My own translation – C.V.J.

2. *Changing Landmarks*: from *Sména vekh*, a volume published in Prague

in 1921 which gave rise to a mainly émigré movement centred on the paper *Nakanúne (On the Eve)*, published in Berlin from 1922. Its members believed that NEP was a first step towards restoring the pre-Revolutionary social structure and that the Bolsheviks should be encouraged to continue the process.

3. *Komchvánstvo*: 'Communist conceit'. See Chapter 3.
4. *Kapitulyánstvo*: 'capitulationising'. See Chapter 3.

APPENDIX V   ON THE REFORMATION OF LITERARY-ARTISTIC ORGANISATIONS

1. My own translation   C.V.J.
2. RAPM: Russian Association of Proletarian Musicians (*Rossiískaya assotsiátsiya proletárskikh muzikántov*).

Selected Bibliography

I GENERAL INTRODUCTORY WORKS IN ENGLISH

Alexandrova, V., *A History of Soviet Literature* (Anchor Books, 1964).

Blake, P., and Hayward, M., *Dissonant Voices in Soviet Literature* (Allen & Unwin, 1962).

Hayward, M., and Labedz, L., *Literature and Revolution in Soviet Russia, 1917–62* (Oxford University Press, 1963).

Simmons, E. J. (ed.), *Continuity and Change in Russian and Soviet Thought* (Harvard University Press, 1955).

——, *Russian Fiction and Soviet Ideology* (Columbia University Press, 1958).

——, *Through the Glass of Soviet Literature* (Columbia University Press, 1961).

Slonim, M., *From Chekhov to the Revolution: Russian Literature 1900–1917* (New York: Oxford University Press, 1962).

——, *Soviet Russian Literature* (New York: Oxford University Press, 1964).

Struve, G., *Soviet Russian Literature* (University of Oklahoma Press, 1951).

II MONOGRAPHS ON MORE SPECIFIC TOPICS IN SOVIET LITERATURE, ETC.

Blake, P. and Hayward, M., *Halfway to the Moon* (Weidenfeld & Nicolson, 1964).

Brown, E. J., *The Proletarian Episode in Russian Literature* (New York, 1953).

Gibian, G., *Interval of Freedom* (University of Minnesota Press, 1960).

Hayward, M., and Crowley, E. L. (eds), *Soviet Literature in the Sixties* (Methuen, 1965).

Markov, Vladimir, *Russian Futurism* (MacGibbon & Kee, 1968).

Mathewson, R. W., *The Positive Hero in Russian Literature* (Columbia University Press, 1958).

Vickery, W. N., *The Cult of Optimism* (Indiana University Press, 1963).

West, James, *Russian Symbolism* (Methuen, 1970).

III ENGLISH WORKS ON ASSOCIATED THEMES

Carr, E. H., *A History of Soviet Russia*, 9 vols. (Macmillan, 1950–69).

Conquest, R. (ed.), *The Politics of Ideas in the U.S.S.R.* (The Bodley Head, 1967).

Deutscher, Isaac, *The Prophet Unarmed* (Oxford Paperbacks, 1970).

Fitzpatrick, Sheila, *The Commissariat of Enlightenment: Soviet Organization and the Arts under Lunacharsky, 1917–21* (Cambridge University Press, 1971).

Huaco, George A., *The Sociology of Film Art* (New York–London: Basic Books Inc., 1965).

Lewin, Moshe, *Lenin's Last Struggle* (Faber & Faber, 1969; translated from French).

Leyda, Jay, *Kino* (Allen & Unwin, 1960).

Nove, Alec, *An Economic History of the U.S.S.R.* (Pelican Books, 1972).

Swayze, Harold, *Political Control of Literature in U.S.S.R., 1946–59* (Harvard University Press, 1962).

Wheeler, Geoffrey, *Racial Problems in Soviet Muslim Asia* (Oxford University Press, 1960).

Wood, Neal, *Communism and British Intellectuals* (Gollancz, 1959).

IV TRANSLATED WORKS

Brézhnev, L., *Lenin's Cause Lives On and Triumphs* (Moscow: Nóvosti Press Agency Publishing House, 1970).

——, *Report of the Central Committee of the Communist Party of the Soviet Union* (Moscow: Nóvosti Press Agency Publishing House, 1971).

Górky, M., *On Literature* (Moscow: Foreign Languages Publishing House).

How the Soviet Revisionists Carry out All-Round Restoration of Capitalism in the U.S.S.R. (Peking: Foreign Languages Press, 1968).

Khrushchëv on Culture (Encounter Pamphlet, No. 9).

Kosýgin, A., *Directives of the Five-Year Economic Development Plan of the USSR for 1971–75* (Moscow: Nóvosti Press Agency Publishing House, 1971).

Krúpskaya, N., *Memories of Lénin* (Panther Books, 1970).

Lénin, V. I., *On Culture and Cultural Revolution* (Moscow: Progress Publishers, 1970).

——, *On Literature and Art* (Moscow: Progress Publishers, 1970).

——, *Questions of National Policy and Proletarian Internationalism* (Moscow: Foreign Languages Publishing House, 1960).

——, *What is to be Done?* (trans. S. V. and P. Utechin), (Panther Books, 1970).

Lukács, G., *Solzhenitsyn* (Merlin Press, 1969; translated from German).

——, *The Meaning of Contemporary Realism* (Merlin Press, 1969; translated from German).

Mao Tse-tung, *On Literature and Art* (Peking: Foreign Languages Press, 1967).

——, *Speech at the Chinese Communist Party's National Conference on Propaganda Work* (Peking: Foreign Languages Press, 1967).

Marx, K., and Engels, F., *Selected Correspondence* (Moscow: Progress Publishers, 1955).

Miliúkov, P., *Outlines of Russian Culture II – Literature in Russia* (New York: A. S. Barnes & Co. Inc., 1942).

Socialist Realism in Literature and Art (trans. C. V. James) (Moscow: Progress Publishers, 1971).

Súslov, N. A., *Inspired by the October Revolution* (Moscow: Nóvosti Press Agency Publishing House, 1970).

Trótsky, Leon, *Literature and Revolution* (Ann Arbor Paperbacks, University of Michigan Press, 1960).

Zhdánov, A. A., *On Literature, Music and Philosophy* (Lawrence & Wishart, 1950).

V RUSSIAN LANGUAGE SOURCES (in cyrillic alphabetic order)

Boguslávskii, A. S., Díyev, V. A., *Rússkaya sovétskaya dramaturgíya, 1946–66* (Moscow: Naúka, 1968).

Bushman, A. S. (ed.), *Naslédiye Lénina i naúka o literatúre* (Leningrad: Naúka, 1969).

Vinográdov, V. V., *et al.* (eds), *Nóvoye o Mayakóvskom* (Moscow: Ak. Naúk S.S.S.R. 1958).

Vneocherednói XXXI s'yezd Kommunistícheskoi Pártiyi Sovétskogo Soyúza. Stenografícheskii otchët.

Vólkov, Zalésskaya, Zalésskii, *Sovétskaya literatúra dlya studéntov inostrántsev* (Moscow: Vysshaya shkóla, 1968).

Vtorói vsesoyúznyi s'yezd sovétskikh pisátelei. Stenografícheskii otchët (1956-.

'*Vysókoye prizvániye*' (*Izvéstiya*, 26 January 1972).

Gróshev, A. (ed.), *Kratkaya istóriya sovétskogo kinó* (Iskússtvo, 1969).

Yershóv, Ye. F. (ed.), *Istóriya rússkogo sovétskogo romána* (Moscow-Leningrad: Naúka, 1965).

'*Zabóta pártiyi obyázyvayet*' (*Literatúrnaya gazéta*, 25 January 1972).

Za vysókuyu idéinost' sovétskoi literatúry (Moscow: Gosizdát khudózhestven noi literatúry, 1959).

Za kommunistícheskuyu idéinost' literatúry i iskússtva (Moscow: Goslitizdát, 1957).

Istóriya Kommunistícheskoi Pártiyi Sovétskogo Soyúza (Moscow: Gospolitizdát, 1960).

Istóriya rússkoi sovétskoi literatúry (Moscow: Ak. Naúk S.S.S.R., 1958).

Istóriya Vsesoyúznoi Kommunistícheskoi Pártiyi (*Bol'shevikóv*), (Moscow: Gospolitizdát, 1938).

Kótov (ed.), *Literatúrnaya Moskvá, sbórnik vtorói* (Moscow: Gosizdát khudózhestvennoi literatúry, 1956).

Kruzhkóv, V. S. (ed.), *Lénin i iskússtvo* (Moscow: Naúka, 1969).

Krúpskaya, N. K., *O Lénine* (Moscow: Izd. politícheskoi literatúry' 1971).

Lébedev, P. I. (ed.), *Iskússtvo, rozhdënnoye oktyabrëm* (Moscow: Sovétskii khudózhnik, 1967).

Lévin, Sh. M., Valk, S. N., Dyákin, V. S., *V. I. Lénin i rússkaya obshchéstvenno-politícheskaya mysl' XIX – nachála XX v.* (Leningrad: Naúka, 1969).

Lénin, V. I., *Anarkhízm i sotsialízm.*

——, *Gosudárstvo i revolyútsiya.*

——, *Zadáchi rússkikh sotsiál-demokrátov.*

——, *Iz próshlogo rabóchei pecháti v Rossíyi.*

Lénin, V. I., *Krestyánskaya refórma.*

——, *Kritícheskiye zamétki po natsionál' nomu voprósu.*

——, *L. N. Tolstói kak zérkalo rússkoi revolyútsiyi.*

——, *Násha blizháishaya zadácha.*

——, *Násha prográmma.*

——, *O sotsiál'noi demokrátiyi v Rossíyi.*

——, *Ot kakógo naslédstva my otkázyvayemsya?*

——, *O Vékhakh.*

——, *Pámyati Gértsena.*

——, *Partíinaya organizátsiya i partíinaya literatúra.*

——, *Pobéda kadétov i zadáchi rabóchei pártiyi.*

——, *Proyékt réchi po agrárnomu voprósu vo vtorói Gosudárstvennoi dúme.*

——, *Chto délat'?*

——, *Chto takóye 'Druz'yá naróda'* . . .

V. I. Lénin o literatúre i iskússtve (Goslitizdát, 1957).

Lénin, V. I., i Gór'kii, A. M. *Pís'ma, vospominániya, dokuménty* (Moscow: Naúka, 1969).

K. Marks i F. Engel's ob iskússtve (Moscow: Iskússtvo, 1957).

Métchenko, A. I., i Polyák, L. M. (eds), *Istóriya rússkoi sovétskoi literatúry* (uchébnoye-posóbiye dlya universitétov), (Izdátel'stvo moskóvskogo universitéta, 1963).

Myasnikóv, A. S., i El'sbérg, Ya. Ye. (eds), *Léninskoye naslédiye i literatúra XX véka* (Izdat. 'Khudózhestvennaya literatúra', 1969).

Sutyágin (ed.), *Osnóvy marksístsko-léninskoi estétiki* (Akadémiya naúk S.S.S.R. (Moscow: Gosizdát. políticheskoi literatúry, 1960).

Pérvyi vsesoyúznyi s'yezd sovétskikh pisátelei. Stenografícheskii otchët.

Prótiv dogmatísma i vul'garizátsiyi v literatúre i iskússtve (Moscow: Politizdát, 1964).

Térekhov, I. M. (ed.), *A. V. Lunachársky – Statyí o sovétskoi literatúre* (Moscow: 'Prosveshchéniye', 1971).

Timoféyev, L. I., i Deméntyev, A. G. (eds), *Rússkaya sovétskoi literatúra*: posóbiye dlya studéntov pedinstitútov (Moscow: Gos. uchébnopedagogícheskoye izdat. Ministérstva prosveshchéniya R.S.F.S.R., 1958).

Trélin, G., *Léninskii lózung 'Iskússtvo – naródu!' i stanovléniye sovétskoi muzykál'noi kul'túry* (Moscow: Izdat. 'Múzyka', 1970).

Trétii s'yezd pisátelei S.S.S.R., 1959. Stenografícheskii otchët.

Fridlender, G., *K. Marks i F. Engel's i voprósy literatúry* (Moscow: Gosizdát 'Khudózhestvennoi literatúry', 1962).

Khrushchëv, N. S., *Za tésnuyu svyaz' literatúry i iskússtva s zhizn'yu naróda* ('Iskússtvo', 1958).

Sheshukóv, S., *Neístovyye revníteli* (Moskóvskii rabóchii, 1970).

VI PARTY STATEMENTS

O Proletkúl'takh (Pis'mó TsK R.K.P., 1.XII.20).

Resolyútsiya po voprósam propagándy, pecháti i agitátsiyi (XII S'yezd R.K.P. (b), 1923).

Resolyútsiya o pecháti (XIII S'yezd R.K.P. (b), 1924).

O politike pártiyi v óblasti khodózhestvennoi literatúry (Resolyútsiya TsK R.K.P. (b), 18.VI.25).

O rabóte Komsomóla v óblasti pecháti (Postanovléniye TsK R.K.P. (b), 14.VIII. 25).

O meropriyátiyakh po uluchshéniyu yúnosheskoi i détskoi pecháti (Postanovléniye Tsk V.K.P. (b), 23.VII.28).

O vystupléniyi chásti sibírskikh literátorov i literatúrnykh organizátsii protiv Maksíma Gór'kogo (Postanovléniye TsK V.K.P. (b), 25.XII,29).

Ob izdániyi 'Istóriyi grazhdánskoi voiny' (iz postanovléniya TsK V.K.P. (b), 30.VII.31).

Ob izdátel' skoi rabóte (Postanovléniye TsK V.K.P. (b), 15. VIII.31).

Ob izdániyi 'Istóriya zavódov' (Postanovléniye TsK V.K.P. (b), 10.X.31).

Ob izdátel' stve 'Molodáya gvárdiya' (Postanovléniye TsK V.K.P. (b), 29.XII.31).

O perestróike literatúrno-khudózhestvennykh organizátsiyi (Postanovléniye TsK V.K.P. (b), 23.IV.32).

Selected Index